ABORTION POLITICS IN THE FEDERAL COURTS

Abortion Politics in the Federal Courts

Right Versus Right _____

Barbara M. Yarnold

Westport, Connecticut
London

Library of Congress Cataloging-in-Publication Data

Yarnold, Barbara M.
   Abortion politics in the federal courts : right versus right /
Barbara M. Yarnold.
      p.   cm.
   Includes bibliographical references and index.
   ISBN 0–275–95291–6 (alk. paper)
   1. Abortion—Law and legislation—United States.   2. Political
questions and judicial power—United States.   3. Abortion—
Government policy—United States—Citizen participation.
4. Abortion—Political aspects—United States.   5. Pro-choice
movement—Political aspects—United States.   6. Pro-life movement—
Political aspects—United States.   I. Title.
KF3771.Y37   1995
344.73′04192—dc20
[347.3044192]   95–6944

British Library Cataloguing in Publication Data is available.

Library of Congress Catalog Card Number: 95–6944
ISBN 0–275–95291–6

First published in 1995

Praeger Publishers, 88 Post Road West, Westport, CT 06881
An imprint of Greenwood Publishing Group, Inc.

Printed in the United States of America

The paper used in this book complies with the
Permanent Paper Standard issued by the National
Information Standards Organization (Z39.48–1984).

10   9   8   7   6   5   4   3   2

To the unloved

CONTENTS

TABLES

PREFACE

I would like to sincerely thank those who made this work possible. In graduate school, I was fortunate to work with two inspiring political scientists, Andrew McFarland and Lettie Wenner. I received a Ph.D. in Public Policy Analysis/Political Science in 1988 from the University of Illinois at Chicago.

I drafted most of this book in my second year as an Assistant Professor of Public Administration at Florida International University, in North Miami, Florida. The reduced teaching load (two courses per semester) assisted me enormously in this endeavor, as well as other material resources and the positive reinforcement of Dr. Allan Rosenbaum, Dean of the School of Public Affairs; Dr. Harvey Averch, Chair of the Department of Public Administration; the support staff at the university; and my friends and colleagues.

Of course, I would not have endeavored upon this work if not motivated by love for humanity. To a great extent, I owe this to my family: Helen Maria Yarnold, my mother; Irena Maria Suszko, my aunt; Susan Maria Yarnold, my sister; and my brothers, Paul Richard Yarnold, Ph.D.; Charles Nicholas Yarnold; James Alexander Yarnold; and Jack Christopher Yarnold.

Also, I dedicate this to the memory of my father, James Knapps Yarnold, Ph.D., a dedicated father and scholar; and to my grandparents, especially Stanislawa and Micolaj Suszko, who labored intensely so that their grandchildren might have a glimpse of hope.

The index and the professional and aesthetic graphs were produced by Cindy Yarnold (a happy new addition to the Yarnold family) and James A. Yarnold, my brother, living in Chicago, Illinois.

I would also like to thank my dear and supportive friends in Florida, especially Leslie Swisher, Melissa Ahern, and Teresa Moloney.

...tion as a Human Right—International and
... Law Review (2008): 249-294. Print.

...esca, Minerva. "After-birth abortion: why should the baby
...cal Ethics (2012): 311-450. Print.

...org, Patricia. Abortion: a positive decision. New York: Bergin & Garvey, 2012.

...nt.

4. Naden, Corinne. Abortion. New York: Marshall Cavendish Benchmark, 2012. Print.

5. Stotland, Nada. Abortion: facts and feelings: a handbook for women and the people who care about them. Washington: American Psychiatric Press, 2008. Print.

ABORTION POLITICS IN THE FEDERAL COURTS

CHAPTER 1

INTRODUCTION

ONE FREQUENTLY HEARS beleaguered politicians leaving political office at all levels decrying the interest-group system that operates in the United States mutilates sound public policies and obstructs all efforts at responsible planning. The discontent with the interest-group system transcends partisan bounds, as officials of both political parties must play the interest-group game or pay the consequences. One wonders what has gone wrong with the naive formula offered by Dahl (1956, 1961) and other "early pluralists" (McFarland 1987), who envisioned an interest-group system that would be fairly representative of most interests and enhance representative government. This naive pluralism was quickly replaced by cynicism as the nation and scholars including, notably, Schattshneider (1960) and Olson (1971), found that the interest-group system was inherently unbalanced, tending always to favor the "haves" over the "have nots."

The troubling conclusion is that public policies will not always be broadly representative of most interests. Instead, those interests that are represented by groups will likely obtain more beneficial public policies than those who are not represented by groups. Invariably, almost any political system, but particularly one that is dominated by a narrow band of groups, will produce arbitrary public policies, and specifically, policies that violate the rights of members of the political community.

In the United States, the remedy for those who are wronged by the political system is provided for by the Constitution, which sets forth a government of separated powers. Specifically, when the political system produces unlawful policies, individuals turn to the federal courts for recourse. Once again, the objectivity of the federal courts is presumably assured by the fact that federal judges have lifetime appointments and are thus immune to political pressures, including those emanating from interest-group lobbying.

However, interest groups may also "bully" the federal courts in their litigation efforts. As I was beginning to do research for this project, I was extracting from official reporters post-*Roe v. Wade* (1973) abortion cases that cite to *Roe* in coming to their decisions (I refer to these cases as the "progeny" of *Roe*). In case after case, and particularly in more recent years, I came across federal district court cases that (almost) mirrored congressional hearings in terms of the number and variety of interest groups that were involved in the proceedings.

For example, in *National Organization for Women v. Operation Rescue*, 726 F. Supp. 1483 (1989), seventeen organizations were involved, sixteen representing the pro-choice position and one, Operation Rescue (the defendant), representing the pro-life position. On the pro-choice side were such organizations as the National Organization for Women (NOW) and its local affiliates, Planned Parenthood affiliates, and nine family-planning and abortion clinics. The decision, incidentally, favored the pro-choice plaintiffs.

Many analysts have documented the fact that judges are subject to political influences in their decision-making and have thus questioned the extent to which the federal courts are actually apolitical (Cook 1981; Wenner 1982; Wenner and Dutter 1988; Baum 1989; Yarnold 1988, 1990a, 1990b, 1991a, 1992a). I am interested to find in this analysis whether interest-group litigation affects judicial outcomes, and to explore the political and litigation-related resources of groups (Chapters 2 and 3).

Also, I am interested in examining whether other political factors are related to outcomes in abortion cases—measured as pro-choice decisions—such as the partisanship of judges (or their appointing presidents) and the preferences of judicial constituents. This analysis also explores whether judicial decisions in abortion cases are related to the region in which the district courts are located (Chapter 2). The next part of the analysis examines whether the litigation success of groups in abortion cases is a result of their repeat-player status (and litigation resources) or their political clout (Chapter 3). The last part of the analysis focuses upon the individual groups, and through survey research I attempt to obtain as much information about them as possible, including the resources of these groups, their political lobbying activities, litigation efforts and strategies, and other similar information (Chapter 4). The conclusion contains overall evaluations of abortion litigation and the participants in this area of policy-making (Chapter 5).

CHAPTER 2

JUDICIAL OUTPUTS

This analysis examines decisions of federal-district courts for the years 1973–1990 in abortion cases that rely upon *Roe v. Wade* as a precedent. An effort has been made to examine whether judicial decisions are significantly related to three political variables: the percentage of Congressmen in judges' states who are female as a measure of a relevant judicial constituency, the partisanship of judges (or more precisely, the partisanship of their appointing presidents), and whether interest groups are involved in litigation. Also included in the analysis is the geographic region in which district courts are located and a "fact" variable: whether the law being challenged in a case is state or federal.

The analysis suggests one political factor, the involvement of pro-choice interest groups in abortion cases, and one regional factor, whether a case is adjudicated in the West, are significantly related to outcome. It is argued that political factors are related to outcomes in abortion cases since: (1) the litigation issues involved in abortion cases are "major," publicized issues; and (2) interest groups, particularly pro-choice interest groups, were heavily involved in abortion litigation. It is also argued that region is significantly related to outcome because of the highly ideological nature of the abortion issue.

Earlier research (Yarnold 1990a, 1990b, 1991a, 1992a) found that region was not a significant factor in court cases dealing with refugees, asylees, and international extradition. In an attempt to reconcile this with even earlier findings that region was, for example, related to outcome in environmental cases (Wenner 1982; Wenner and Dutter

1988), and race-relations cases (Richardson and Vines 1978), I suggested that regional effects might be most apparent in judicial cases that deal with a highly ideological issue. Abortion was cited as one type of case in which it was anticipated that federal-court judges might exhibit regional differences in their decision-making.

This analysis examines the extent to which federal-district-court judges, in their decisions in abortion cases from 1973 to 1990, have served to enhance the abortion rights of women, first given protection by the Supreme Court in *Roe v. Wade*, 410 U.S. 113 (1973). It also examines the extent to which these decisions are related to political, factual, and regional variables.

HYPOTHESES

Though the judiciary is often viewed as a passive interpreter of "the law," federal court judges examined in this analysis were not unduly restrained in their decision-making by the law, due to the vagueness of standards they were called upon to interpret. In abortion cases decided from 1973 to 1990 that rely upon *Roe v. Wade* (1973) as a precedent (*Roe*'s progeny), federal district courts were required to apply the holding of *Roe* to state and federal laws being challenged and to determine whether they had unconstitutionally infringed upon abortion rights. However, as is often the case in judicial decision-making, there is great ambiguity in the language of *Roe*; hence, there are few standards that bind judges to employ uniform criteria in their decision-making.

In order to comprehend the *Roe* decision and the controversy it engendered, one must examine first the precedent upon which *Roe* relied, which set forth the privacy right. This precedent is the Supreme Court's decision in *Griswold v. Connecticut*, 381 U.S. 479 (1965). This case arose when Griswold, the executive director of Planned Parenthood League of Connecticut, was convicted under a state statute that made the use of contraceptives a criminal offense and also punished accessories who, like Griswold, provided information, instruction, and advice to married couples in order to prevent pregnancies through contraception. Joined as a codefendant was a professor of Yale Medical School, who served as medical director of Planned Parenthood League of Connecticut. According to one account (Garraty 1987), Planned

Parenthood had been attempting to change the state law banning contraceptives for decades, but had been successfully opposed by a powerful block of Catholic state legislators who halted all efforts at reform.

An initial observation is that powerful interest groups in the United States were affected by the Supreme Court's decisions in *Griswold* (*Roe*'s precursor) and in *Roe* as well. These groups played a role in shaping the Supreme Court's agenda and rulings in both cases, and undoubtedly benefited from their litigation exposure and experience in this issue area, which derived from decades of involvement in privacy and abortion-related litigation.

The defendants in the *Griswold* case were confronted with some difficulty since they admitted violating the state law in question. In order to avoid prosecution, the defendants claimed the state law violated their privacy rights protected by the due-process clause of the Fourteenth Amendment. However, as Justices Black and Stewart suggested in their dissent, there is no explicit privacy right set forth in the Constitution. The defendants countered by arguing that the privacy right was an implicit right that emanated from "penumbras" found in certain provisions of the Bill of Rights. In one of the most problematic cases ever faced by law students in their relentless search for "black letter law," the Supreme Court, in an opinion delivered by Justice Douglas, recognized the right to privacy and held that it was violated by the state statute that banned the use of contraceptives. A portion of that opinion is as follows:

> The foregoing cases suggest that specific guarantees in the Bill of Rights have penumbras, formed by emanations from those guarantees that help give them life and substance.
> . . . Various guarantees create zones of privacy. The right of association contained in the penumbra of the First Amendment is one. . . . The Third Amendment in its prohibition against the quartering of soldiers "in any house" in time of peace without the consent of the owner is another facet of that privacy. . . . (*Griswold v. Connecticut*, 381 U.S. 479, 1965).

By the time this paragraph concludes, the Court cited the First, Third, Fourth, Fifth, and Ninth Amendments in its search for the extra-constitutional privacy right and, in the process, created a new constitutional lingo that sent legal scholars in search of "penumbras." Nevertheless, for the purposes of *Roe* and pro-choice litigation groups, *Griswold* set forth the important precedent that a constitutional right of privacy exists.

By the time that *Roe* reached the Supreme Court in 1973, a strong pro-choice coalition had formed in the United States consisting of groups of medical professionals who had been, in some cases, performing abortions in violation of the law and sought to legalize the practice; also involved were women's-rights organizations, civil-liberties groups, and population-control groups, among others (Garraty 1987). The opposition, consisting primarily of conservative religious groups, was not well organized at this point.

In 1973 the Supreme Court in *Roe v. Wade*, 410 U.S. 113, and the companion case of *Doe v. Bolton*, 410 U.S. 179, in reliance on the privacy right set forth earlier in *Griswold*, held that the Fourteenth Amendment due-process clause and the "privacy right" had been violated by Texas and Georgia laws that banned abortions except where necessary to save the mother's life (Texas law), or where the pregnancy would endanger the life of the mother or seriously injure her health (Georgia law). The immediate result of this ruling was that the abortion laws of forty-six states and the District of Columbia were invalidated (Wolpert and Rosenberg 1990).

Justice Blackmun drafted and delivered the opinion in *Roe v. Wade* (1973) that was supported by seven members of the Supreme Court. Justice Blackmun recognized that the state of Texas had a legitimate interest in regulating abortions to protect both maternal and fetal life. However, state interests had to be weighed against the privacy interests of women, which accorded them the right to the termination of an early pregnancy. In Blackmun's words: "We therefore conclude that the right of privacy includes the abortion decision, but that this right is not unqualified and must be considered against important state interests in regulation. . . ." (*Roe v. Wade*, 1973).

Hence, the decision was ultimately based upon the Supreme Court's resolution of the issue of when a state's interest in protecting maternal and fetal life becomes sufficiently compelling to warrant state regulation of abortion. The state law, it will be recalled, banned all abortions unless necessary to save the life of the mother. In response to the issue of the state interest in maternal life, the decision states:

With respect to the State's important and legitimate interest in the health of the mother, the "compelling" point, in light of the present medical knowledge, is at approximately the end of the first trimester. This is so because of the now established medical fact . . . that until the end of the first trimester mortality in abortion is less than mortality in normal childbirth. It follows that, from and after this point, a State may regulate the abortion procedure to the extent that the regulation reasonably relates to the preservation and protection of human health (*Roe v. Wade*, 1973).

Hence, future judges, when considering the legitimacy of a law that regulates post-first-trimester abortion enacted to foster maternal health, are called upon to determine if the regulation "reasonably relates" to its stated goal; this is certainly a vague standard.

Even more problematic is the determination as to when a state's interest in protecting fetal life becomes compelling. In response to this, the opinion reads: "With respect to the State's important and legitimate interest in potential life, the 'compelling' point is at viability. This is so because the fetus then presumably has the capability of meaningful life outside the mother's womb" (*Roe v. Wade*, 1973). Earlier, based upon medical testimony, Blackmun had concluded that "viability is usually placed at about seven months (28 weeks) but may occur earlier, even at 24 weeks. . . ." Before viability, or during the first trimester of pregnancy, states are severely limited in their ability to regulate abortions: "If the State is interested in protecting fetal life after viability, it may go so far as to proscribe abortion during that period except when it is necessary to preserve the life or health of the mother" (*Roe v. Wade*, 1973).

Hence, courts are given the rather vague message that pre-first-trimester regulation is highly suspect, yet after this point, regulation may be acceptable if "necessary to preserve the life or health of the mother." Distinguishing between laws that meet this post-first-trimester standard and those that do not is indeed a formidable task.

In making the determinations as to when a fetus becomes viable and whether maternal life is more endangered by childbirth than abortion, the Supreme Court was, of course, entirely dependent upon expert testimony. Expert testimony during the action on both issues, but particularly on the question of fetal viability, was massive and conflicting (Garraty 1987).

Some believe that the Supreme Court should not attempt to make determinations that greatly rely upon scientific and medical expertise, such as whether the fetus is viable (Blank 1984). As one commentator suggests:

It is argued here that the courts are put in a difficult position when they base decisions on biological rationale, especially when they fail to recognize or understand the extent to which technological advances are altering biological "fact." These controversies have an "inherently hybrid technical and legal character" and "present issues that can be resolved by neither purely technical nor purely legal analysis." . . . These issues force the courts to deal not only with new forms of information but also with new methods of analysis for understanding causality which are totally alien to the language and mode of analysis of the legal profession. It is not surprising, therefore, that these new demands on the courts produce severe strain as well (*Blank 1984*: 584–85).

It should come as no surprise, given the vagueness of the underlying standards for abortion cases, that judicial decisions have been attacked as arbitrary and, in some cases, even biased. Of course, many critics contend that abortion is a highly politicized issue (Hildreth 1990). As a result, they suggest that judicial decisions relating to abortion are not immune to political pressure. For example, Sackett (1985) asserts that the Supreme Court issued a decision in *Roe v. Wade* that paralleled public preferences.

As a result of their discretion, courts substitute their own standards for vague legal and constitutional standards. Hence, federal court outcomes may be related to variables that have little to do with the "law" or the "facts" of a case. The following discussion reviews several extraneous independent variables drawn from public-law research that have been found in previous analyses to be related to judicial outcomes.

POLITICAL VARIABLES

Political variables may be significantly related to district court outcomes in abortion cases. This suggestion may seem anomalous since federal courts are generally viewed as immune to political influences since their members have been appointed for life and socialized into objectivity. However, in the same way that courts have been shown to engage in policy-making and not merely legal interpretation, many analysts concede that judicial decision-making is often linked to political factors. Judges do not operate in a vacuum and so may be influenced by their environment, including their political environment. Hence, judicial outcomes have been linked to such political factors as the involvement of groups in litigation, the partisan affiliation of judges, public opinion, and constituency preferences.

From earlier analysis, it is expected that federal court outcomes will be linked to political factors in two types of cases: (1) where the issue is "major" and publicized and on which constituents have preferences that serve to restrict policy-makers (Yarnold 1990a, 1990b, 1992a); and (2) where the litigation issue is not a major one, yet affects the interests of politically powerful groups within the United States (Yarnold 1991a, 1992a).

POLITICAL PARTY

If judges are influenced by political variables, perhaps district court outcomes in abortion cases are related to the partisan affiliation of the judges involved or the partisan affiliation of their appointing presidents (Baum 1989; Goldman 1975; Nagel 1961; Vines 1963; Yarnold 1990a, 1990b, 1991a, 1992a; Carp and Rowland 1983). Since the Supreme Court's ruling in *Roe v. Wade* (1973), the Republican Party has identified itself with an anti-abortion stance, whereas Democrats were quick to adopt a pro-choice position (Appleton 1981; Horan 1981; Segers 1982; Granberg 1985; Bolce 1988). Although Republican politicians tended to drift into the "pro-choice" camp toward the end of the 1980s, abortion may still be an issue that leads to partisan division. Hence, it is expected that Democratic judges will more likely enter a "pro-choice" ruling in abortion cases than Republican judges.

INTEREST-GROUP LITIGATION

Interest groups "lobby" the courts through their direct involvement in litigation (Yarnold 1990a, 1990b, 1991a, 1992a). As such, another "political variable" that many assert affects federal court outcomes is the involvement of organized interests in litigation. In the federal district court abortion cases included in this analysis, two categories of interest groups became involved, either as *amicus curiae* or as representatives: (1) "pro-choice" interest groups; and (2) "pro-life" interest groups. The analysis examines the extent to which the involvement of "pro-choice" versus "pro-life" interest groups in litigation affects the outcome in abortion cases or leads to a decision that is "pro-choice."

JUDICIAL CONSTITUENCIES AND PUBLIC OPINION

Other political variables that may have an impact on judges are public opinion (Cook 1981; Baum 1989) and the preferences of "judicial constituents" (Yarnold 1990a, 1990b, 1991a, 1992a). When evaluating the link between policy-making and constituency preferences, one must address the question of which constituency of the decision-maker might be most directly affected by the decision in question (Yarnold 1990a, 1990b, 1991a, 1992a). In abortion cases, the constituency most likely to be affected by judicial decisions consists of women.

As Scott and Schuman (1988) suggest, pro-choice women regard the abortion issue as more important than pro-choice men since it is women, both individually and collectively, who stand to lose most by abortion restrictions. Similarly, for those who oppose abortion, the Supreme Court's grant of legal sanction to this practice is viewed as a threat to traditional morality and the family unit (Petchesky 1984; Luker 1984; Clarke 1987; Scott and Schuman 1988). Hildreth (1990) suggests that abortion might be an issue on which women coalesce. Hence, women may be a significant judicial constituency in abortion decisions. The presence of a politically powerful female constituency in judges' states may influence judicial outcomes.

One way to assess the political clout of women in states is to measure the percentage of federal Congressional seats (for both the Senate and the House) that are held by women (in the year in which a decision is rendered). I expect that district court judges from states with a high percentage of Congresswomen will more likely adopt a "pro-choice" position in abortion cases than judges in states with a low percentage of Congresswomen. This variable was obtained by combining data on women in Congress provided by the Center for the American Woman and Politics (CAWP, National Information Data Bank on Women in Public Office, Eagleton Institute of Politics, Rutgers University) and *Congressional Quarterly* (1988, 1973–1990).

COMPETING HYPOTHESES

Although conceding that courts are policy-makers unconstrained by the "law" and "facts" of a case, other analysts suggest that court outcomes are linked to environmental variables, and that environmental variables explain as much or more of the variance in judicial outcomes as political variables.

REGION

Geographic region has often been cited as a contextual variable that affects judicial decision-making. Carp and Rowland (1983) show that judicial decisions in the South and West were more conservative than those rendered by their counterparts in the North and Midwest. Richardson and Vines (1978) point out that judges in the South were least sympathetic to civil-rights litigants. Cook (1978) discovered that the most severe sentencing decisions were rendered by federal district judges located in the South. Wenner (1982) also found that in environmental litigation, region was related to judicial decision-making. Later, Wenner and Dutter (1988) suggest that region continued to affect these outcomes and that in district court cases involving environmental litigation, pro-environment groups enjoyed the most support from judges in the Northeast (circuits 1, 2, and 3), followed by judges in the Midwest (circuits 6, 7, and 8). Lower levels of support were exhibited by judges in the South (circuits 4, 5, and 11); judges in the West (circuits 9 and 10) were divided in their support of pro-environment groups. Hence, a first competing hypothesis is that geographic region is significantly linked to judicial outcomes in the abortion cases involved in this analysis.

FACT VARIABLE: STATE VERSUS FEDERAL LAW

It has also been suggested that judicial outcomes are related to the important "facts" of a case (Segal 1985; Gibson 1977; Dudley 1989;

Gryski et al. 1986; Haire and Songer 1990). One fact that may be important in abortion cases is whether the abortion law being challenged is a federal or state policy. Some analysts suggest that the activism of the federal judiciary is more apparent when state (rather than federal) laws are being challenged, as evidenced by the fact that state laws are overturned by the federal judiciary at a much higher rate than their federal counterparts (Baum 1989). Hence, this variable is included as a second control variable.

DATA AND METHODS

Data for this analysis consists of the "progeny" of *Roe v. Wade*, 410 U.S. 113 (1973), or federal district-court cases decided after that landmark case was entered by the Supreme Court that cite to *Roe* in coming to their decisions. The district court cases included were decided between January 22, 1973, the date of the Supreme Court's decision in *Roe*, and the end of 1990. These cases were found in the *Federal Supplement*, an official source for federal district court cases. A total of 145 cases is included in the analysis. An additional case was excluded from the analysis because it was decided by the District of Columbia district court and hence could not be properly coded on the region variable.

The dependent variable is whether the decision is "pro-choice," broadly construed as a decision that promotes the abortion rights of women as set forth in *Roe v. Wade* (1973). This is a dichotomous variable, which suggests that standard regression analysis with its assumption that the dependent variable is continuous is not appropriate for these purposes. Although most of the cases were presided over by one judge, in some cases, the panel included up to three judges.

The first independent variable, the partisan affiliation of judges or, more precisely, the partisan affiliation of their appointing presidents, is measured as follows: high/low percentage of judges involved in a district court case who were appointed by a Democratic president. This variable has been dichotomized at its mean: 47 percent of all judges involved in the 145 district court cases were appointed by a Democratic president. One complication that arises is that, as mentioned, some of these cases were decided by only one judge whereas others were decided by a panel of up to three judges. For the purposes of measurement, when one district court judge is presiding and was appointed by a Democratic president, this case is coded on the partisanship variable as follows: "100 percent of judges appointed by Democratic president." If three judges are presiding, and one of the judges were appointed by a Democratic president, this case is coded as: "33 percent of judges appointed by Democratic president."

The involvement of interest groups in the federal district court abortion cases is measured by examining the written decisions for each one of these cases, which typically list whether interest groups are involved. The groups that are involved are then coded in terms of whether they are "pro-choice" or "pro-life." Interest groups are included whether they appear in a representative capacity or as *amicus curiae*.

To assess the strength of women as a judicial constituency, a measure was taken of the percentage of Congressmen (including both Senators and Representatives) in a judge's state (or more precisely, in the state in which the district court is located) who were female in the congressional session (from the 93rd Congress to the 101st, covering the years 1973–1990) during which the decision was rendered. The data on Congresswomen was obtained from CAWP. The data on the congressional delegations of individual states were found in reports on Congress (*Congressional Quarterly* 1988; 1973–1990).

Statistical analysis consists of probit analysis, since the dependent variable, whether the decision is pro-choice, is continuous and there are multiple independent variables. Probit analysis enables one to examine the relationship between multiple independent variables and a dependent variable when controlling for the other variables. Probit analysis has been successfully employed in earlier analyses of judicial decision-making (Yarnold 1990a, 1990b, 1991a, 1992a; Wenner and Dutter 1988; Segal 1984).

FINDINGS: RELATIONSHIPS BETWEEN DISTRICT COURT ABORTION DECISIONS AND THE INDEPENDENT VARIABLES

After the insignificant regional variable of "South" is deleted, the results of probit analysis are in Table 2.1 (see page 15).

The only statistically significant independent variables are: the involvement of pro-choice groups in litigation (p = .005) and the location

Table 2.1

Profit Estimates For District Court
Abortion Cases, 1973-1990

Dependent Variable: Was Decision Pro-Choice?

Mean: 77%

Variable	Maximum Likelihood Estimate (M.L.E.)	Standard Error (S.E.)	M.L.E./S.E.
Constant	5.24	0.65	8.03
High % Democratic Judges	0.05	0.25	0.20
Pro-Choice Groups	0.77	0.25	3.02**
Pro-Life Groups	-0.07	0.42	-0.16
High % Women In Congress	-0.30	0.26	-1.16
Region			
Court in North	-0.39	0.43	-0.91
Court in Midwest	-0.62	0.40	-1.54
Court in West	-1.00	0.53	-1.90*
State Crime	0.71	0.49	1.45

Chi Square = 32.08   D.F. = 34   p = .56
N = 145

* Significant at 0.05.
** Significant at 0.005.

of a district court in the West (p = .05), one political variable and one regional variable. The overall equation lacks statistical significance (p = .56).

With regard to the insignificant variables, most of the results conform with earlier speculation about the direction of the relationships between the independent variables and district court outcomes in abortion cases. Hence, Democratic judges (or judges appointed by Democratic presidents) were more likely to take a pro-choice position in their rulings, the involvement of pro-life groups in litigation tended to decrease the likelihood of a pro-choice decision, and the fact that a case involved state rather than federal law increased the probability that the law would be found unconstitutional.

But there were surprises. The presence of a high percentage of Congresswomen in a judge's state decreased, not increased, the probability that judges in that state would take a pro-choice position. These findings, therefore, suggest that judges did not take into account the possibly pro-choice positions of politically powerful women in their states. Alternately, the measure of this judicial-constituency variable may be flawed or the position of women on the abortion issue may be divided between pro-choice and pro-life camps, thereby giving no clear direction to policy-makers, including judges.

Other surprises were that pro-choice litigants were damaged when their cases were presided over by district courts located in the North (insignificant), Midwest (insignificant), and West (significant). Earlier probit analysis with the South included suggests that only this regional variable has a positive relationship with the dependent variable. Pro-choice litigants were more likely to win in the South and were likely to face the greatest opposition from, in descending order, judges from the West, Midwest, and North.

The analysis reveals that pro-choice court decisions are linked to the involvement of pro-choice groups and the location of district courts in the West. Judicial outcomes, however, were not significantly related to other "political" variables: the partisanship of judges (or that of their appointing presidents), the involvement of pro-life groups in litigation, and the presence of a politically powerful group of Congresswomen in judges' states (as a measure of a judicial constituency in abortion cases).

Other facts about these cases warrant inspection. Most notable is the huge involvement of interest groups, both pro-choice and pro-life, in these cases: 66 percent of the cases (96 out of 145) had interest-group involvement. However, the pro-life forces were overwhelmed by the much higher involvement of pro-choice groups. Pro-choice groups were involved in 65 percent (or 94 out of 145) of the cases, as compared to only 10 percent (or 14 out of 145) for pro-life groups. Hence, pro-choice groups enjoyed a 6.5 to 1 advantage over pro-life forces, which was linked to highly favorable court outcomes for the pro-choice forces. A pro-choice decision was entered in 77 percent (111 out of 145) of the abortion cases.

Pro-choice groups appear to have a very well-organized—and

funded—litigation strategy and benefit from cooperative litigation efforts among pro-choice women's groups, groups of health-care providers who often have a financial interest in liberal abortion laws (such as abortion clinics), and civil-rights groups. For example, a pro-choice position was often advocated by local affiliates of the American Civil Liberties Union (ACLU) and the Center for Constitutional Rights, both broadly based civil liberties organizations that serve as watchdogs of the civil rights of all groups in the United States, not only women.

Other groups specifically dedicated to the protection of women's rights were also quite active in these cases, such as NOW. Associations of health-care providers also were involved, aware by now of the enormous risks illegal abortions pose to women and of their own increasing financial stake in the provision of abortions; many local abortion clinics and groups of health-care providers became advocates of women in these cases, as well as more powerful national organizations, including Planned Parenthood, the National Medical Association, the National Association of Social Workers, and the American Public Health Association. Still other groups were also involved, though not with as great frequency, in making pro-choice arguments, including such various religious organizations as the Religious Coalition for Abortion Rights and such pro-bono legal services providers as New Hampshire Legal Assistance.

Earlier research (Yarnold 1990b, 1991a, 1992a) found that success in litigation is significantly linked to cooperative litigation efforts by interest groups. Undoubtedly, pro-choice forces enjoyed this advantage in federal-court abortion cases examined in this analysis. This advantage was not, however, shared by pro-life groups. While it was not at all unusual to have more than one group involved in an abortion case on the pro-choice side, appearances by pro-life groups tended to be solo appearances, with a small number of groups representing the pro-life side. The same pro-life groups tended to surface in these cases: the Constitutional Right to Life Committee, Operation Rescue, Advocates for Life, Celebrate Life, Americans United for Life Legal Defense Fund, along with various ad hoc or local groups, such as Minnesota Citizens for Life, the Georgia Right to Life Committee, and Christians in Action. Most often, however, pro-life groups did not appear in these cases.

Another statistically significant variable is West region (p = .05).

Courts in the West tended to rule against litigants who were advocating a pro-choice position. However, only 8 percent (n = 12) of the abortion cases were decided in the West. The South was also underrepresented in these cases; only 16 percent (n = 23) of the abortion cases were adjudicated by courts in the South. More than two-thirds of the cases were decided in the Midwest (47 percent, n = 68), and the North (29 percent, n = 42), where pro-choice arguments were not always success-ful. However, given that 94 percent of the cases (or 136 out of 145) involve a challenge to state law and that the pro-choice position pre-vailed in 77 percent of all cases, the "typical case" was one decided in a district court in the Midwest or North, which involved pro-choice interest groups who mounted a successful challenge to a state abortion law. Hence, it appears that federal district court judges throughout the United States were very active in these abortion cases in whipping policy-makers and judges in the Midwest and North into conformity with the national norm for abortion rights set forth by the Supreme Court in *Roe v. Wade* (1973).

DISCUSSION

Statistical analysis reveals that two variables are significantly related to outcome in federal district court abortion cases decided from January 22, 1973, the date of the Supreme Court's historic ruling in *Roe v. Wade* (1973), to 1990. One of these variables is a political one: the involve-ment of pro-choice interest groups in litigation. This political variable increased the probability that judges would enter a pro-choice decision in the abortion cases examined in this analysis. Federal court outcomes in these cases were also significantly linked to one regional variable: the location of the federal court in the West.

From earlier analysis, it was expected that federal court outcomes will be linked to political factors in two types of cases: (1) where the issue is "major" and publicized and on which constituents have prefer-ences that serve to restrict policy-makers (Yarnold 1990a, 1990b, 1991a, 1992a); and (2) where the litigation issue is not a major one, yet affects the interests of politically powerful groups within the United States (Yarnold 1991a, 1991b, 1992a). Both of these conditions are met in the context of abortion cases. First, abortion is a "major" issue, if one defines a "major" issue as one that is "institutionalized in party cleavages and linked to broad ideology among the public, where opinions are fairly firmly held and information about congressmen [judges] is easily obtainable" (*Page et al. 1984*: 753).

In fact, the abortion issue did lead to deep partisan division in the United States. After the 1973 decision of the Supreme Court in *Roe v. Wade*, the two major parties adopted opposing positions on abortion in 1976, with Democrats on the pro-choice side and Republicans supporting a pro-life position (Bolce 1988; Granberg 1985). By 1980, the difference sharpened between the Republican and Democratic Party platforms on the abortion issue (Bolce 1988). Ronald Reagan, the 1981 presidential nominee of the Republican Party, was regarded as staunchly pro-life and supported by pro-life groups, including the National Right to Life Committee. Then-President Jimmy Carter, the Democratic nominee, was committed to a pro-choice position (Granberg 1985). George Bush, the Republican candidate for President, called for a constitutional amendment banning abortion in April 1989; Governor Dukakis, the Democratic nominee, was strongly pro-choice (*The Economist*, 1989).

From the above, it appears that the abortion issue is "institutionalized in party cleavages" (Page et al. 1984) and from this perspective qualifies as a major issue. It also is an issue that is "linked to broad ideology among the public, where opinions are fairly firmly held" (Page et al. 1984), and information about decisions of policy-makers is readily available. Graber (1990) suggests that the abortion issue is linked to broad public conceptions about the proper role of women in society: homemaker versus career woman. The availability of abortions, according to some abortion critics, promotes promiscuity and hence endangers the traditional homemaker role of women. Others (Johnson et al. 1990) agree, noting that the abortion movement that arose in the United States was divided on cultural grounds, with traditionalists bitterly opposed by libertarians.

By 1980, abortion had been legal for more than seven years, yet it remained controversial (Granberg 1985). According to some commentators, legalized abortion was the most explosive and polarizing issue of the 1980s (Bolce 1988; Blank 1984). One goes even further, suggesting that abortion continues to be an issue that "once or twice in a century

. . . arises so divisive in nature, so far-reaching in its consequences, and so deep in its foundation that it calls every person to take a stand" (*Blank 1984*: 585).

Even if abortion were not a major issue, one might expect federal court outcomes in abortion cases to be politicized because of the existence of numerous interest groups, both pro-choice and pro-life, which are affected by decisions in these cases. In fact, the collective action of interest groups around the abortion issue led to the development of first a vigorous pro-life movement in the early 1980s, followed by the resurgence of a powerful pro-choice movement toward the end of the 1980s.

Sackett (1985) describes the Supreme Court's rulings in *Roe v. Wade*, 410 U.S. 113 (1973) and the companion case of *Doe v. Bolton*, 410 U.S. 179 (1973), as a great shock to pro-life forces in the United States, which were less than organized in 1973. She adds that these twin rulings, which had the effect of sanctioning abortion on demand, moved many interest groups in the United States to band together to protest what seemed to be the Court's outrageous and immoral act.

From 1973 through the 1980s, the pro-life movement was in the ascendency as the movement attracted the support of established religious organizations, women's groups, other groups, and elected politicians. It also led to the formation of new public-interest groups, such as Women Abused by Abortion. One commentator suggests that the "powerful, relentless march forward by the pro-life movement has been one of the political phenomena of the eighties" (*Woodman 1989*: 21). In fact, the pro-life movement managed to corner the pro-choice movement into a position of defensiveness (Woodman 1989). The tactics of groups active in the pro-life movement ranged from minor civil disobedience, such as the picketing of abortion clinics (*The Economist*, 1989), to the actions of "fringe groups" in the social movement (Yarnold 1991b), such as Operation Rescue, whose members bombed thirty-two clinics, set fire to thirty-eight clinics, issued death threats to clinic workers, and harassed women at abortion clinics during the 1980s (Woodman 1989; Cockburn 1989).

The pro-life coalition had some policy successes in the 1980s as state and local governments became involved in placing limits on abortion. As mentioned earlier, Republican Presidents Reagan (1981–1989) and Bush (1989–1993) were both committed to a pro-life position. Congress made many attempts in the 1980s to weaken the Supreme Court's decision in *Roe v. Wade* (1973), including congressional attempts to eliminate public funding of abortion (Appleton 1981; Horan 1981) and pass a Human Life Statute or Amendment to the Constitution (Segers 1982).

The efforts of the pro-life movement also met with an important judicial victory in the 1989 case of *Webster v. Reproductive Health Services*, which served to severely limit women's access to abortions (Woodman 1989). Specifically, the Supreme Court allowed Missouri and thus state governments in general to ban the use of public hospitals and other facilities supported by public funds for the performance of nontherapeutic abortions (a nontherapeutic abortion is not necessary to save a woman's life). The Supreme Court also upheld the right of Missouri to ban public employees from participating in abortions and substantially increased the costs of an abortion by sanctioning that part of state law that required doctors to perform a battery of tests after twenty weeks of pregnancy to determine if the fetus could survive outside of the mother's womb (Cockburn 1989).

Pro-life groups were temporarily emboldened by the Court's decision in *Webster* and engaged in a vigorous campaign to push through state and federal laws restricting abortion (*The Economist*, 1989). The *Webster* decision of 1989 however, had the much more significant effect of mobilizing a strong backlash against the pro-life lobby (Woodman 1989). Some commentators suggest that the Court's ruling in this case galvanized the pro-choice movement and led to its resurgence at the end of the 1980s (*The Economist*, 1989). In fact, on April 9, 1989, 300,000 pro-choicers converged on Washington (Woodman 1989). Their efforts were coordinated by existing groups, such as NOW (Cockburn 1989). This, in turn, led to the formation of new pro-choice groups. A researcher describes the new, revitalized pro-choice movement and its membership:

> The women's movement now vows to create a storm across the country in defense of abortion rights. Pro-choice people who in the past voted their conservative economic interests never expecting that anything could unhinge abortion rights which they considered established are now beginning to have second thoughts. The cautiously liberal National Organization for Women is planning to launch nationwide caravans modelled on

the civil rights movement's freedom rides and to hold demonstrations that violate the law. Women who have never attended a protest march in their life are travelling to distant cities and filling the streets in their own towns (*Cockburn 1989*: 19).

The above discussion demonstrates that the abortion issue intimately affects the concerns of powerful interest groups in the United States and even led some of these groups to coalesce into the strong pro-life movement of the 1980s, followed by the ascendancy of the pro-choice movement by 1989. Hence, federal court outcomes in abortion cases are politicized not only because abortion is a "major issue," but also because the litigation issue deeply affects the interests of powerful pro-life and pro-choice groups in the United States.

Lending strong support to this argument is the fact that the only significant political variable in the federal district court abortion cases was the involvement of pro-choice interest groups in litigation. Other political variables, such as the partisan affiliation of the judges (or their appointing presidents), the preferences of judicial constituents (here defined as politically powerful Congresswomen within judges' states), and the involvement of pro-life interest groups, did not seemingly affect judicial decision-making in abortion cases.

Upon closer inspection of interest-group involvement in abortion litigation, one of the most striking observations is the overwhelming involvement of interest groups in the abortion cases considered in this analysis: 66 percent of the abortion cases had interest-group involvement. Further, pro-choice groups enjoyed a 6.5 to 1 advantage over pro-life forces in terms of their involvement in these cases, and met with considerable litigation success: a pro-choice decision was entered in 77 percent of the cases. Hence, the involvement of pro-choice interest groups in litigation seems to have had the effect of fostering lower-court implementation of the Supreme Court's ruling in *Roe v. Wade* (1973). Of course, it is difficult to assess whether the district courts were responding to the political clout of these groups or their superior capabilities in litigation (Yarnold 1990a, 1990b, 1991a, 1992a); it was likely a combination of the two.

Earlier research (Yarnold 1990b, 1991a, 1992a) linked litigation success to cooperative litigation efforts by interest groups. In the abortion cases examined, pro-choice interest groups not only had numerical superiority in terms of appearances in district court cases, but also had the major advantage of engaging in joint litigation with other similar groups that shared their pro-choice position on the abortion issue.

The pro-choice position was strengthened through the multiple representation it received in the federal courts as diverse groups came to advocate a pro-choice position. For example, pro-choice arguments were made in these cases by pro-choice women's groups, groups of health-care providers that have a financial stake in liberal abortion laws, broadly based civil-liberties groups, and even in some instances, by religious organizations. Further, these groups often banded together in abortion cases, engaging in quite effective joint litigation strategies.

In spite of their broader power in the United States political scene, pro-life groups shared none of the advantages of pro-choice groups when it came to litigation before the federal district courts. Specifically, pro-life litigation was sporadic (only 10 percent of the cases involved pro-life groups as opposed to 65 percent for the pro-choice position), did not have the benefit of multiple representation by different groups with similar interests, and showed little evidence of cooperative litigation efforts among pro-life groups. Appearances by pro-life groups tended to be solo appearances, with a small number of groups representing the pro-life position. It is not altogether surprising that the federal courts adopted a pro-life position in only 23 percent of the abortion cases.

While reading earlier analyses (Yarnold 1990a, 1990b, 1991a, 1992a), I found that region was not significantly related to court outcomes in federal-court cases involving claims for political asylum and withholding of deportation and requests for international extradition. In an attempt to reconcile these analyses with earlier research that found a relationship between region and judicial outcomes in environmental cases (Wenner 1982; Wenner and Dutter 1988) and race-relations cases (Richardson and Vines 1978), it was argued that regional effects might be most apparent in those types of cases that involve a highly ideological issue.

In accordance with this argument, region is significantly related to the outcome in the federal court abortion cases examined here. Specifically, West region is the significant regional variable, and cases decided by courts in the West tended to go against the pro-choice position at a higher rate than cases decided by judges located in district courts in the Midwest, North, and South.

To find evidence of the highly ideological nature of the abortion issue in the United States, one need look no further than daily press coverage, which chronicles the intensity of the battle between pro-choice and pro-life forces, the effect the abortion issue has had on political campaigns throughout the country, and the massive mobilization of individuals into pro-life and pro-choice movements (*The Economist*, 1989). One commentator aptly categorizes abortion as an issue that: "once or twice in a century . . . arises so divisive in nature, so far-reaching in its consequences, and so deep in its foundation that it calls every person to take a stand" (*Blank 1984*: 585).

Instead of passively interpreting the "law" and the "facts" of abortion cases, the federal courts were dealing with a major issue that mobilized citizens and interest groups into a battle with a high level of intensity and ideological content. These courts were not immune to their larger political and environmental context, but became directly involved in making critical decisions on abortion rights that had the potential of generating intense hostility and controversy. In the process, the courts responded to a political factor, the involvement of pro-choice interest groups in litigation, and to their regions.

Overall, it must be said that the federal courts did not, in abortion cases, shirk their responsibilities through procedural technicalities—for example, not many cases were dismissed on the basis that litigants lacked standing—but instead actively pursued their policy-making function. These decisions, 77 percent of which adopted a pro-choice position, served to collectively reinforce the Supreme Court's ruling in *Roe v. Wade* (1973), which gave recognition to the abortion rights of women. The lower federal courts, for the most part, served to foster implementation of the *Roe* decision.

Of course, the burden of this federal-court policy-making was not equally borne by all. The "typical" abortion case was decided in a district court in the Midwest or North and involved pro-choice interest groups that mounted a successful challenge to a state abortion policy. Federal district court judges, thus, for the most part, were activists when it came to state policy and, through their decisions in abortion cases, whipped law-makers and judges in the Midwest and North into conformity with the national norm for abortion set forth in *Roe v. Wade* (1973).

CHAPTER 3

Do Courts Respond to the Political Clout of Groups or to Their Superior Litigation Resources/Repeat-Player Status?

THE TRADITIONAL EXPLANATION for the high levels of success typically enjoyed by interest groups has been that these groups are "repeat players" in litigation (Galanter 1974, 1978; Dolbeare 1978; Epstein 1985; Wenner 1982; Wenner and Dutter 1988; Yarnold 1990a, 1990b, 1991a, 1992a; Baum 1989, 1990). Organizations, as repeat players in litigation, tend to prevail more often in court cases than individuals, who are not typically involved in litigation. Even when individuals are represented by a private attorney, they are unable to match an organization's advantages in litigation. One advantage organizations have is that they gain experience and expertise in litigation that can be used to effectively argue the merits of a case (Vose 1959; O'Connor 1980).

Another litigation advantage enjoyed by certain types of organizations, particularly public-interest organizations, is their extensive interaction with similar groups, through which these groups exchange information and ideas about the best litigation strategies. The intergroup exchanges may be relatively informal, including sending representatives of their groups to conferences attended by representatives of other, similar groups. At the formal end of the continuum is joint litigation, in which groups join efforts, usually with the intent of affecting policy change through litigation (Baum 1990; Yarnold 1990a, 1990b, 1991a, 1992a).

Another reason that organizations may have an advantage in litigation is that their continuous inputs to the courts may have induced the courts, over time, to change the governing rules to their advantage (Galanter 1974, 1978; Yarnold 1990a, 1990b, 1991a, 1992a). Still another alternate explanation for the interest-group advantage in litigation, and an explanation that has been only indirectly (Baum 1989, 1990) or cautiously (Wenner and Dutter 1988) suggested in public-law literature, is that courts, in favoring interest groups in litigation, are responding to the political clout of these litigants and not to their superior litigation capabilities. As a junior scholar in the field, I was one of the few who incautiously adopted this argument (Yarnold 1988, 1990a, 1990b, 1991a, 1992a).

Why, after all, should federal court judges, who have the security of lifetime appointments, respond to political forces, such as interest-group litigation? I earlier argued that federal court judges, before their appointment to the judiciary, tend to be political activists so that an appointment to the federal bench is often a reward for earlier political service (Yarnold 1988, 1990a, 1990b, 1991a, 1991b, 1992a). Baum (1989) notes the activist pasts of members of the federal judiciary, many of whom have held positions as state court judges, occupied administrative posts, or even held elective political office.

Another factor that contributes to the politicization of the federal judiciary is that many federal court judges were actively involved in partisan politics before their appointment. It is not surprising, therefore, that the partisan affiliation of judges is an important factor in the selection of the federal judiciary (Schmidhauser 1978; Goldman 1975;

Nagel 1961; Vines 1963; Carp and Rowland 1983; Yarnold 1992a). Presidential appointees to the federal bench are overwhelmingly members of the same political party as the President (Baum 1989; 1990; Yarnold 1992a).

Even if sincere attempts are made to shield federal judges from political forces, the federal judiciary is continuously exposed to a court environment that attracts powerful political actors (Baum 1989; Yarnold 1992a). The same interest groups that dominate policy-making by the legislative and executive branches (Schattshneider 1960; Olson 1971; Lowi 1979; McFarland 1980) are present in the federal courts, though their lobbying of the federal judiciary is constrained somewhat by the formality and symbolism of the institution, both of which tend to wrap the judiciary in an aura of nobility, objectivity, and impartiality. These judicial formalities lead, for example, to rules that prohibit interest groups from lobbying the federal judiciary through normal political channels; interest groups cannot, for example, offer to finance a federal judge's campaign or have *ex parte* communications with a presiding judge (Baum 1989, 1990; Yarnold 1992a). Appropriate lobbying of the federal judiciary by organized interests is through interest-group litigation or the active involvement of groups in cases (Baum 1989, 1990; Yarnold 1992a).

Not surprisingly, much of the public-law research conducted on this issue found that interest-group litigation is significantly linked to judicial outcomes, and that interest groups tend to prevail in federal court litigation (Galanter 1974, 1978; Dolbeare 1978; Epstein 1985; Wenner 1982; Wenner and Dutter 1988; Yarnold 1988, 1990a, 1990b, 1991a, 1992a). Judicial outcomes appear to be quite sensitive to the positions taken by groups in court cases. In fact, interest groups may very well influence judicial policy-making as much as they do executive and legislative policy-making (Wenner and Dutter 1988; Yarnold 1990b, 1992a).

Other political factors that, simply due to their presence, serve to imbue the federal courts' environment with a distinctly political character, include representatives of federal, state, and local government who are routinely involved in federal court litigation (Baum 1989; Yarnold 1992a).

My addition is that federal court judges continue to decide cases in a politicized manner "due to the prospect of future promotion within the ranks of the judiciary or appointment to administrative positions" (Yarnold 1990a, 1992a). After investing enormous effort and time into laying the necessary foundations for a successful career, federal court judges, particularly those in district courts and circuit courts of appeal, are likely still plagued by high levels of ambition and energy. Whether these processes take place at a conscious or unconscious level (Yarnold 1992a), federal court judges have been found to be responsive to public opinion (Cook 1977), constituent demands (Richardson and Vines 1978; Giles and Walker 1978; Yarnold 1988, 1990a, 1990b, 1991a, 1992a), their partisan affiliations (Schmidhauser 1978; Goldman 1978; Nagel 1961; Vines 1963; Atkins 1972; Walker 1972; Levin 1978; Yarnold 1988, 1990a, 1990b, 1991a, 1992a), interest-group litigation (Galanter 1974, 1978; Dolbeare 1978; Epstein 1985; Wenner 1982; Wenner and Dutter 1988; Yarnold 1988, 1990a, 1990b, 1991a, 1992a), and a number of other political factors.

For all of these reasons, the ostensibly apolitical federal judiciary responds to political pressures. As summarized at an earlier time, federal judges have been conditioned, because of their pre-appointment activities, "to serve as political actors, that is, to be responsive to the subtle pressures from their political environment" (Yarnold 1992a: 9). In short, there are many incentives that drive federal court judges to respond to political factors.

Returning then to the focus of this section, the question that must still be dealt with is, to the extent that federal-court judges respond to interest-group involvement in federal-court cases as one of a number of political factors, are these judges reacting to the litigation resources of these groups or to their political clout? Although there is some indirect support for the hypothesis that courts respond to the political power of groups (Baum 1989, 1990; Yarnold 1992a), there has not been, to my knowledge, any direct test of the "politics" versus "repeat-player" dichotomy.

Two of the greatest obstacles to testing whether courts respond to the repeat-player status of groups and the superior litigation resources they bring to federal court cases or to the political power of groups are the difficulties involved with devising measures of whether particular inter-est groups are repeat players in federal court cases, and determining the litigation resources of these groups. These obstacles, however, seem undaunting when compared to the more major difficulty of devising a test of whether a particular group is politically powerful. What types of activities (or resources) make a group politically powerful? On a practical level, is it possible to obtain information about the political activities of groups; is it likely, for example, that they will divulge such information in response to a survey?

In spite of these obstacles, the challenge here is to devise, employing for this purpose an appropriate set of federal court cases, adequate measures of whether a group is a repeat player, the litigation resources of interest groups, and the political clout of groups that are involved in federal court cases.

FINDING THE "RIGHT CASE" BY APPLYING A GENERAL MODEL OF PUBLIC LAW

The first task in the pursuit of testing whether courts respond to the litigation resources/repeat-player status of groups or to their political power is to find the "right type" of case. In these circumstances this is a case in which federal court judges might respond to the political power of groups, or one in which federal court outcomes may be politicized because of the nature of the issue considered by the courts.

In earlier research, Cook (1977) discovered that judicial outcomes were linked to public opinion in draft-evasion cases. I found that adjudicative outcomes were not related to political factors when the case involved criminal sentencing (Yarnold 1992a) and when the case was an administrative appeal to the Board of Immigration Appeals (BIA) from denials of applications for political asylum and withholding of deportation (Yarnold 1988, 1990b, 1990a, 1992a). Nevertheless, in other federal court cases dealing with refugees and asylees (Yarnold 1988, 1990a, 1990b, 1992a), international extradition (Yarnold 1991a, 1992a), and abortion (Yarnold 1992a), I found that court outcomes were significantly related to political factors.

From this point, I devised a "general model of public law" that explains these conflicting findings on the extent to which judicial outcomes are linked to political factors (1992a). Specifically, I predict, "courts, whether their members are appointed or elected, are expected to respond to their political environment when (1) the case affects the interests of powerful interest groups in the United States; and/or (2) the issue involved in the case is a major, publicized one" (Yarnold 1992a:

105). The political factors that I predict may affect judicial decision-making include the partisanship of the judges adjudicating a case or the partisanship of the presidents who appointed them, the preferences of judicial constituents, and the involvement of interest groups in cases (Yarnold 1992a).

Therefore, in order to test whether courts respond to the political clout of groups or their litigation resources/repeat-player status, the best type of case would be one in which the issue the court deals with is major and publicized and a case in which interest groups are deeply interested in judicial outcomes. Abortion cases meet both criteria. Many commentators suggest that the abortion issue is highly politicized (Hildreth and Dran 1990). In my own research, I found that federal court judges responded in abortion cases to the involvement of pro-choice groups in litigation (Supra, Chapter 2; Yarnold 1992a). For these reasons, this analysis focuses upon abortion cases decided by the federal courts.

HYPOTHESES: FACTORS RELATED TO LITIGATION SUCCESS BY GROUPS

A broader theme of this discussion is to explore factors related to litigation success by interest groups. Although many scholars have addressed this issue, few have organized or categorized these variables in any meaningful way. It is suggested that variables related to litigation success can be grouped into three general categories: (1) litigation-related variables, where the variable in question affects the interest group in its litigation efforts; (2) political variables, where the interest group has certain political characteristics and/or activities that distinguish it from other groups; and (3) generic organizational variables, which range from merely descriptive accounts of group characteristics to more meaningful measures of the organization's strength or cohesiveness.

LITIGATION-RELATED VARIABLES

A first litigation-related variable (LR) is whether the group is a repeat player in litigation. As Galanter (1974, 1978) points out, groups that make repeated use of the courts have an advantage over those who make only rare appearances. Hence, the inquiry that must be made is rather straightforward: whether groups are frequently involved in court cases.

One of the resources interest groups bring to court is financial resources sufficient to sustain them through protracted litigation (Epstein 1985; O'Connor and Epstein 1983; Yarnold 1988, 1990b, 1991a, 1992a; Vose 1990). Hence, a second LR is that groups have large budgets.

Vose (1959) notes that groups tend to be more successful in litigation as well as more successful in changing judicial policy when they have longevity. O'Connor (1980) also finds that the National Consumers League was able to ensure that favorable legislation was implemented because of that group's longevity, which enabled it to play an effective watchdog role and make repeated forays into the courts. Others agree that longevity is an important advantage to participants in interest-group litigation (Epstein 1985; O'Connor and Epstein 1983). However, in one analysis involving legal organizations that provided pro bono or low-cost assistance to refugees and applicants for political asylum, longevity actually impaired the groups' chances of prevailing in federal court cases (Yarnold 1988, 1990b), while "new" organizations—those formed in or after 1980—were more likely to prevail. The explanation was that new groups might attract highly zealous and idealistic staff members: "Perhaps public interest groups, like government agencies, lose enthusiasm for a policy goal over time" (*Yarnold 1990b*: 193). Nevertheless, longevity is considered to be an LR.

A fourth LR of interest groups is their staff size. The larger the staff, the more likely it is that the organization has highly trained specialists who contribute in various ways to litigation efforts, providing, for example, secretarial services, legal services, and investigatory services. Of course, staff size is directly related to the financial resources of groups, so it is not surprising that success in litigation is linked to the number of staff members available to interest groups (Yarnold 1988, 1990b).

O'Connor (1980) suggests in her review of the National Consumers League that the group's success in court was partly attributable to the fact that it maintained control over the conduct of particular cases. Related to this is Epstein's (1985) observation that interest groups prefer to directly sponsor court cases instead of filing *amicus-curiae* briefs since this enables the groups to choose test cases and create the record for appeal. In contrast, my (1988, 1990b) analysis of public legal-interest groups finds that the variable of direct sponsorship of cases is not significantly related to court outcome. Nevertheless, the argument that groups gain some measure of control over litigation by directly sponsoring cases seems plausible, so I include this as another LR of groups.

Related to direct sponsorship of cases by groups, which helps to reduce the chance of surprise in litigation efforts, is the litigation purpose of the group. Groups may pursue litigation with the goal of helping a particular litigant or changing legal precedent, and sometimes their approach to court cases combines the two goals. In all likelihood, the narrow result-oriented litigation goal of helping a particular litigant is easier to accomplish by groups than the more ambitious undertaking of changing legal precedent, which may take decades of concerted effort on the part of groups (Vose 1959; O'Connor 1980). Hence, an additional LR of groups may be their narrow focus in litigation efforts, so that their purpose is simply to help a litigant and not to effect a change in legal precedent.

A seventh LR is whether interest groups cooperate with other, similar groups. Epstein and O'Connor (1983; Epstein 1985) and others suggest that a major advantage of groups is their cooperation with similar groups. Hence, the seventh LR measures simply whether groups cooperate with each other generally. LR variables eight through ten measure the precise nature of this cooperation, starting from less formal methods of cooperation to more formal ones. LR eight is concerned with whether groups regularly exchange information with other similar groups. LR nine measures whether groups send representatives to conferences and seminars attended by representatives of other groups. LR ten is at the high level of the formality continuum, measuring whether groups engage in joint litigation, which has been shown to increase the probability of success by groups in litigation (Yarnold 1988, 1990b). The last LR, number eleven, examines whether groups engage in high levels of inter-group cooperation.

POLITICAL VARIABLES

Political variables (POLs) are factors that may be related to the litigation success of interest groups that measure the political characteristics and/

or activities of groups. Of course, underlying this is an attempt to assess the "political clout" of groups, as discussed earlier.

From previous analysis of federal court abortion cases (Supra, Chapter 2; Yarnold 1992a), where the courts ruled in favor of pro-choice interest groups at a statistically significant level, one anticipates that the political ideology of groups involved in abortion litigation will be linked to success in litigation. In the abortion cases, groups fell into two categories, those that are pro-choice and those that are pro-life (Supra, Chapter 2; Yarnold 1992a). One expects that a pro-choice political ideology will be significantly related to success in cases dealing with the abortion issue. Hence, the first POL is the political ideology of the group, and specifically, whether a group is pro-choice.

The second POL is referred to as "politic" and measures whether the organization is highly involved in political processes. In order to determine whether an organizational litigant has political power, one must examine its political activities. Baum (1989, 1990) and others (Yarnold 1988, 1990a, 1990b, 1991, 1992a; Vose 1990) note that interest groups are quite active in lobbying Congress on judicial appointments. Hence, when one devises a measure of the political clout of groups, an obvious question is whether the groups lobby Congress on judicial appointments and if so, how frequently?

Similarly, since it has been argued that campaign contributions made by groups buys them access to lawmakers and that this access is often equal to influence (Schlozman and Tierney 1986; Berry 1989), another part of the "politic" measure is whether the group contributes money to congressional campaigns and if so, how frequently. Groups lobby on many issues aside from judicial appointments, so another component of the "politic" variable is whether the group testifies before Congress and, if so, how often? And since group lobbying also extends to bureaucracy (Baum 1989, 1990; Yarnold 1988, 1990b; Berman 1988; Bryner 1987; Rosenbloom 1989), a fourth part of the "politic" measure examines whether the group meets with agencies with regard to proposed rules and regulations. If political pressures count, then a group that is highly involved in the political process (and is labeled here as "politic") should have more favorable judicial outcomes than groups with a low measurement on this variable.

The next set of POLs relate to the identity of the interest group, which may or may not affect judicial outcomes in abortion cases. The organizations that appeared in these cases fall into the following categories:

a. public interest
b. civil liberties
c. religious
d. abortion clinics affiliated with Planned Parenthood
e. for-profit abortion clinics not affiliated with Planned Parenthood
f. nonprofit abortion clinics not affiliated with Planned Parenthood
g. women's rights
h. professional associations and unions
i. legal aid
j. public hospitals (note: there is only one of these).

Hence, the three major POLs include the political ideology of the groups (whether they are pro-choice), whether the groups are very involved in the political process in the United States, and the identity of the groups that are involved in abortion cases.

GENERIC ORGANIZATIONAL VARIABLES

Generic organizational variables (ORGs) range from mere descriptions of the groups to more insightful measures of organizational strength or cohesiveness. The first ORG is whether the group uses volunteers in its day-to-day operations. The use of volunteers by an organization, particularly one with limited resources, may expand the operating capacity of the group with minimal investment in training volunteers. If an organization is able to attract volunteers, this may also be an indication of that group's popularity with the general public.

The second ORG is concerned with the main source of funds for the organization whether from fees, membership dues, donations, support from the government (federal, state, or local), or grants.

DATA AND METHODS

Federal court abortion cases were already identified as an appropriate data set for the purpose at hand, namely testing the extent to which courts are responsive to either the political power of groups or their litigation resources. Part of the data collection has already been completed. This analysis employs the same data set of federal court cases that were used earlier to analyze federal district court outcomes in abortion cases (Supra, Chapter 2; Yarnold 1992a). The cases included are the progeny of *Roe v. Wade*, 410 U.S. 113 (1973) or federal district court cases decided since the date of *Roe*, January 22, 1973, which rely upon *Roe* in their decisions and are included in the *Federal Supplement*, an official source for federal district court cases. The cutoff date was the end of 1990, and there are a total of 145 cases included in the original data set.

The second part of the analysis was a great deal more labor-intensive. Initially, all of the 145 cases were scanned, and a list of all organizations involved in the abortion cases was compiled. After obtaining an organizational list with 166 different organizations that became involved in the abortion cases, I needed to obtain the addresses and telephone numbers of the various organizations. Next, I drafted a survey in an attempt to gather information from these organizations on their litigation resources, political activities, and general organizational characteristics (see Appendix A). I then mailed the survey to the leaders of these organizations.

The initial mailing had disappointing results, with only about 7 of the 166 groups returning a completed survey. These efforts were followed by telephone surveys that continued for approximately seven months, from October 1991 to April 1992. Much of the delay stemmed from the fact that the survey asked groups to divulge potentially harmful confidential information about their political activities and litigation efforts. Private abortion clinics were particularly reluctant to provide the requested information, openly expressing concern over the possibility of disruption of their activities by members of the pro-life movement and needing reassurance about my identity and purpose. Other groups had similar reservations. Of all the surveys I had conducted to this point, this one was the most demanding. I eventually obtained completed surveys for 126 of the 166 organizations, a response rate of 76 percent.

After obtaining information about the political and legal resources of groups, I moved on to the next part of the project: to return again to the 145 *Roe* district court cases and to compile a list of the federal court cases each of the 166 organizations became involved in, whether the organization itself was supporting a pro-choice or pro-life position in each case, and whether the organization's position prevailed in each case it appeared in. With aggregate information about each group's success in the abortion cases it participated in, I was then able to measure each organization's success rate in litigation, which I measured as "percentage wins in all abortion cases for organization."

Although surveys were completed for 126 of the organizations, other information about these groups was listed in the district court cases. This included the identity of the group, for example, whether it was an abortion clinic. The political ideology of the groups, whether pro-choice or pro-life, was also apparent from the opinions in the abortion cases because groups allied themselves with either a pro-choice or pro-life position. As such, when no survey was completed for a group, in most cases, some background information on the groups was still available. The final data set thus includes all 166 of the organizations that appeared in the *Roe* cases (Yarnold 1992a), although, as mentioned earlier, a completed set of information is available only for 126 of the organizational litigants.

Since this analysis seeks to determine whether district-court outcomes in abortion cases decided between 1973 and 1990 are linked to the political, litigation-related, and organizational variables discussed in the "Hypotheses" section, the dependent variable in this case is the percentage wins in abortion cases for each organizational litigant. The independent variables are all of the POLs, LRs, and ORGs set forth earlier. Statistical analysis consists of regression analysis since the dependent variable is continuous and there are multiple independent variables.

FINDINGS: RELATIONSHIPS BETWEEN INTEREST-GROUP WINS IN ABORTION CASES AND THE POLITICAL/ LITIGATION-RELATED VARIABLES

After deleting some of the independent variables that were shown to be insignificantly related to outcome in earlier regression runs—such as whether the group is a public hospital, a non-Planned Parenthood for-profit clinic, a non-Planned Parenthood nonprofit clinic, and whether the group's main source of funds is grants—I recorded the results of the multiple-regression analysis in Table 3.1 (see pages 37–38). For coding

Table 3.1

Regression Estimates For Wins By Organizational Litigants In Abortion Cases, 1973-1990

Dependent Variable: Percentage Wins for Organization in all Abortion Cases

Mean = 81%

Variable	B	SE B	BETA	T	SIGN T
LR Variables					
Repeat Player	-4.83	10.67	-.06	-.45	.65
Budget	5.11	2.22	.05	.23	.82
Age (longevity)	-.04	.12	-.04	-.35	.73
Staff Size	-.01	.01	-.24	-.83	.41
Direct Sponsor	-.06	11.87	-6.50	-.01	.99
Help Litigant	12.81	11.70	.13	1.09	.28
Cooperate	-76.09	36.66	-.41	-2.08	.04*
Exchange Information	28.46	31.72	.24	.90	.37
Attend Seminars	-4.50	13.83	-.05	-.32	.75
Joint Litigation	34.88	27.07	.45	1.29	.20
High Cooperation	-19.85	28.26	-.26	-.70	.48
POL Variables					
Pro-Choice Ideology	19.55	17.14	.15	1.14	.26
Politic	-17.90	8.15	-.24	-2.20	.03*
Type Of Group					
Civil Liberties	41.17	22.16	.44	1.86	.06**
Planned Parenthood	28.54	17.45	.29	1.64	.10**
Womens' Rights	29.90	24.42	.18	1.22	.22
Professional/Union	14.06	21.35	.11	.66	.51
Religious	5.52	20.52	.06	.27	.79
Public Interest	3.27	23.70	.03	.14	.89
Legal Aid	-16.14	48.18	-.11	-.34	.74
ORG Variables					
Volunteers	16.88	26.79	.06	.63	.53
Source Of Funds					
Government	33.29	48.25	.26	.69	.49
Dues	-13.43	23.32	-.15	-.58	.57
Fees	-14.94	23.02	-.15	-.65	.52
Individual Donors	-33.82	22.61	-.45	-1.50	.14
Constant	93.99	43.11	2.18	.03	

Table 3.1 (Cont.)

**Regression Estimates For Wins By Organizational Litigants
In Abortion Cases, 1973-1990**

N = 166	Adjusted R Square = .22	Analysis of Variance
Multiple R = .65	Standard Error = 33.44	Regression DF = 25
R Square = .42		Residual DF = 69
		F = 2.03
		P = .01

* Significant at the .05 level (or below).
** Significant at .10 level (or below).

<u>Key</u>

LR	litigation resources (variables)
POL	political (variables)
ORG	organizational (variables)
Repeat Player	frequently involved in federal court cases
Direct Sponsor	group always participates only as a direct representative/sponsor in litigation
Help Litigant	primary litigation goal of group is to help litigant (not change legal precedent)
Cooperate	whether groups cooperate with each other
Exchange Information	whether groups exchange information with similar groups
Attend Seminars	whether groups attend seminars attended by representatives of similar groups
High Cooperation	whether groups have a high level of cooperation with other groups
Politic	whether the organization is highly active in the political process

of the variables "politic," (above average levels of political activity by groups), "hicoop" (high levels of cooperation between groups), and "freqlit" (whether the groups were frequently involved in federal court litigation), see Appendix B.

DISCUSSION

The results of the statistical analysis are more dramatic than expected. A rather striking observation is the relatively small contribution made by LRs and ORGs in explaining litigation success by interest groups in abortion cases, while POLs clearly take the lead in terms of their ability to predict litigation success. Hence, in response to the initial inquiry, federal-court outcomes and organizational success seem to be sensitive to political pressures, not to the fact that a group is a repeat player in litigation and as such has superior litigation resources. The overall equation is significant (p = .01) and the variance explained (without adjustments) is 42 percent.

Whether the organization was a repeat player (or had repeated contact with the federal courts) was not significantly related to litigation success (p = .65). In fact, in contrast to the predictions of Galanter (1974, 1978) and others on this matter, when one controls for all of the other factors, being a repeat player actually impaired an organization's ability to obtain a favorable court decision. Repeat players were almost 5 percent more likely to lose in federal court litigation than non-repeat players.

A second litigation resource variable that is not related to the success rate of groups in federal court litigation is the financial position of litigants. Although analysts have linked favorable court outcomes to the financial resources of groups, which enable them to engage in costly, extended litigation (Epstein 1985; O'Connor and Epstein 1983; Yarnold 1988, 1990b, 1991a, 1992a; Vose 1990), this variable is unrelated to litigation success by groups (p = .82).

As in cases dealing with political refugees and asylees (Yarnold 1988, 1990b), organizational longevity is not linked to success in litigation by organizations (p = .73). This finding counters those of others, such as Vose (1959), who suggests that the National Association for the Advancement of Colored People (NAACP) benefited from longevity because of the increased expertise of its legal staff over time, and O'Connor's (1980) more recent examination of the National Consumers League. In this analysis, groups involved in abortion cases were actually at a disadvantage in relation to other groups if they had longevity.

Although Yarnold (1988, 1990b) found a relationship existed between staff size and judicial outcomes, this finding was not replicated here. Staff size is unrelated to litigation success by organizational litigants involved in abortion cases (p = .41). Also insignificantly related to outcome is whether the organizational litigant maintains direct control over the conduct of particular cases whether through direct sponsorship of cases (p = .99) or through having the limited litigation purpose of merely helping a litigant instead of changing judicial policy (p = .28). Note, however, that groups whose litigation purpose was merely to help litigants were close to 13 percent more likely to prevail in abortion litigation than other groups that sought to change judicial policy or had a mixed litigation strategy. These findings contradict both O'Connor

(1980) and Epstein's (1985) predictions that these variables improve an organization's chances of prevailing in litigation.

The only LR that is significantly related to organizational success in abortion cases is inter-group cooperation (p = .04). While Epstein and O'Connor (1983; Epstein 1985) predicted that groups would more often prevail as a result of this cooperation, this analysis shows that general cooperation between groups led to a much greater probability (76 percent) that groups will lose in abortion litigation.

With regard to the specifics of this cooperation between groups, joint litigation, although not significantly related to outcome, did help organizational litigants; those that engaged in joint litigation were almost 35 percent more likely to prevail in abortion cases than those that did not, which supports Yarnold's (1988, 1990b) earlier findings. When groups engaged in informal exchanges of information, they were almost 29 percent more likely to prevail than those groups that failed to exchange information, though this variable is not statistically significant (p = .37). Whether a group sent representatives to seminars attended by other group representatives is not significantly related to outcome either (p = .75).

In contrast, the analysis reveals that POLs seem to be closely related to interest-group success in litigation. However, not all of the hypothesized POLs are significantly related to success in litigation. It was earlier predicted that the pro-choice ideology of a group would be significantly related to litigation success; however, after one controls for other variables, the pro-choice ideology factor is not significantly related to success in litigation (p = .26), although being pro-choice helped litigants in abortion cases; the probability of success increased by almost 20 percent when a group had a pro-choice ideology.

As predicted, significantly related to litigation success is the "politics" variable (p = .03), which evaluates the political clout of groups by examining the extent to which the groups engage in the following activities: lobbying Congress on judicial appointments, lobbying Congress generally, giving money to finance Congressional campaigns, and meeting with agencies with regard to rules and regulations. However, instead of being helped in their litigation efforts by these political activities, the groups that were heavily involved in politics tended to be penalized in the abortion cases examined here; the probability of prevailing in litigation decreased by almost 18 percent for those groups that were highly involved in extrajudicial political activity.

Among the most successful litigants were civil liberties groups (p = .06). Also significant (p = .10) is a group's affiliation with the national organization Planned Parenthood. This affiliation increased a group's chances of prevailing in court cases by almost 29 percent. Also receiving favorable outcomes from the federal courts in abortion cases were, in descending order, women's rights organizations (p = .22), professional organizations and labor unions (p = .51), religious organizations (p = .79), and, lastly, public-interest groups (p = .89); however, none of these is statistically significant. The only groups that were more likely to lose in federal court abortion cases because of their identity were legal-aid groups, although again this variable is not significant (p = .74).

ORGs contribute almost nothing to explaining organizational success in litigation. As predicted, the fact that an organization made use of volunteers in its operations tended to contribute to organizational success in litigation, although this variable is not significant (p = .53). With regard to the source of funds of the organizations, having some level of government as a main source of funds tended to help litigants (p = .49), while a group's primary reliance upon membership dues (p = .57), fees (p = .52), and individual donors (p = .14) tended to hurt organizations in their litigation efforts in the federal courts; once again, though, none of these variables is statistically significant.

Clearly, successful interest-group litigation in abortion cases is linked primarily to POLs, with civil-liberties groups and abortion clinics associated with Planned Parenthood receiving the most favorable outputs from the federal courts, when one controls for other factors. Successful litigation was also significantly linked to an organization's involvement in politics, although politically active groups were penalized for this in terms of court outcomes. Also, for the one LR that is significantly related to litigation success, inter-group cooperation, the relationship is a negative one. This suggests that cooperative efforts among groups hurts rather than helps organizational litigants.

The general picture that emerges indicates that in post-*Roe v. Wade* (1973) abortion cases the federal courts were not responsive to LRs of groups and even their repeat player status. Instead, court outcomes in abortion cases were linked to POLs with civil-liberties groups and Planned Parenthood affiliates obtaining preferential decisions by the federal courts.

CHAPTER 4

ORGANIZATIONAL PLAYERS IN ABORTION LITIGATION IN THE FEDERAL COURTS

PRO-CHOICE GROUPS

According to comments made during extensive interviews lasting from October 1991 to April 1992, the pro-choice camp has been weakened in its lobbying efforts by the existence of an internal split between groups promoting the public interest and those concerned foremost with their economic interests. This split has weakened the pro-choice movement. The pro-life movement, on the other hand, tends to be composed of public-interest groups that have little economic interest in the non-availability of abortions, and tends to be more unified, with the leaders of pro-life organizations promoting similar ideological positions.

One from the pro-choice camp is Bill Baird, who is associated with Parents Aid Society, Inc., of Hempstead, New York (a pro-choice public-interest group), and a longtime advocate of women's rights: he filed the case of *Eisenstadt v. Baird*, 405 U.S. 434 (1972), which was eventually decided by the Supreme Court. In an interview dated November 24, 1991, Baird remarked that the pro-abortion movement had been rendered ineffective at times because of the conflict among groups active in the pro-abortion movement. According to Baird, groups that had emerged as major actors in the pro-choice camp by the 1990s were initially opposed to legalized abortion and even fought to limit the availability of birth control. For example, in the early 1960s the leaders of Planned Parenthood were opposed to both birth control and abortion. They successfully fought Baird's standing to sue in the Supreme Court case that bares his name, *Eisenstadt v. Baird*, 405 U.S. 434 (1972). Planned Parenthood only gradually changed its position on both abortion and birth control.

Currently, Planned Parenthood plays a major role in the pro-choice movement and is an adamant proponent of both birth control and abortion. Baird contends that the pro-abortion movement is currently dominated by Planned Parenthood and other groups that promote the abortion rights of women because of the "profit motive." He points to the fact that Planned Parenthood, for example, until recently received huge subsidies from the federal government. Other abortion clinics and medical professionals who perform abortions clearly have an economic interest in the availability of abortions. While it is helpful to the pro-choice movement to have these economically powerful and politically visible groups arguing in favor of the abortion rights of women, Baird contends that these groups have also, on occasion, taken positions that actually impair these rights when these groups have a major economic interest at stake.

For example, Baird claims that he and others vigorously fought in favor of state and federal policy changes that would allow women to obtain abortions from individuals who are not medical doctors, but who would receive extensive training in safe abortion practices. Such a measure would have the obvious effect of lowering the cost of abortion and simultaneously increasing its availability. Baird claims that these types of initiatives have been repeatedly blocked by the "profit-motivated" medical profession that has worked with Planned Parenthood to ensure that only medical professionals are permitted to perform abortions.

Baird also accuses Planned Parenthood of attempting to gain a monopoly over the provision of abortion and family-planning services. This is based on Baird's observation that the "typical pattern" of Planned Parenthood is to go into a new geographic area and open a clinic near a preexisting abortion clinic that is independent of Planned Parenthood. According to Baird, because Planned Parenthood is a recipient of large federal grants, it is able to provide abortions at a much lower fee than a private abortion clinic can. Hence, over the course of time, the preexisting private abortion clinic, unable to compete with the lower fees offered by Planned Parenthood affiliates, is forced to go out of business.

In my own research, when I attempted to send surveys to private abortion clinics from 1991 to 1992, I was surprised to find how many had been dissolved by the time I attempted to contact them. Baird claims that by these and other similar strategies, Planned Parenthood and medical professionals have worked together to limit the availability of abortions and establish something of a monopoly over the provision of abortions. Of course, medical professionals and Planned Parenthood officials might respond to Baird's charges by suggesting that they seek merely to ensure that abortion services are relatively safe and afford-able. Another factor that Baird suggests has weakened the pro-abortion movement has been a power struggle by the primarily female leadership of some organizations, such as Planned Parenthood, to exclude men from leadership positions in these organizations.

In spite of the apparent disunity in the pro-choice camp discussed by Baird and others, the pro-choice cause is actually more unified than the above comments suggest. Pro-choice groups, unlike the pro-life opposi-tion, gain representation from many different public and private organi-zations. In addition, and this, too, is an advantage not shared by the pro-life movement, the pro-choice side gains dual representation from national and statewide coalitions of similar ideological groups. For ex-ample, in the early part of the 1990s, such groups as local affiliates of the ACLU and Planned Parenthood throughout the United States worked together in national and statewide coalitions for reproductive-freedom rights. Also, the rift between pro-choice public-interest groups and pro-choice private-interest groups is not as great as Baird and others would lead you to believe. For example, the ACLU and its local affiliates, clearly public-interest organizations, regularly work with private pro-choice groups, including Planned Parenthood and medical professionals.

In the following discussion, pro-choice organizations that became involved in cases dealing with abortion since *Roe v. Wade* (1973) are divided into two groups: public-interest groups, including general public-interest groups, civil-liberties groups, religious organizations, and legal-aid clinics; and groups whose pro-abortion position enhances their economic interests, such as Planned Parenthood and its affiliated groups, abortion clinics not affiliated with Planned Parenthood, medical professionals, and other professional groups.

PUBLIC-INTEREST GROUPS

Throughout pluralist literature and your everyday life, you frequently encounter the term "public interest." Unfortunately, what the "public interest" is at any given time is a subjective evaluation, as is the implied second part of the equation, namely, what the "public interest" requires in the form of action or inaction (the course more often taken). Andrew McFarland warns political scientists and others to avoid the danger of "public interest singularity" (*McFarland 1980*: 37), or the mistaken notion that on any one public-policy issue there is only one obvious public interest to examine, which most often just happens to be, coincidentally, the one raised by its proponent.

In light of these observations, can I advance somehow to the more difficult task of defining "public-interest groups," or is this a frivolous task that I should abandon? Fortunately, I am assisted enormously by the work of Olson (1971), Berry (1989), McFarland (1980, 1983) and others (Yarnold 1988, 1990). One definition that I find useful in my discussions of public-interest groups draws upon the distinction between public- and private-interest groups and is as follows: private-interest groups produce collective goods (from their organizational activities) that are intended to benefit only group members (Yarnold 1988, 1990). In contrast, public-interest groups do not intend that only group members share the collective benefit of the groups' activities.

As such, a public-interest group is nonexclusive in terms of the intended beneficiaries of the organization's activities; group members may also share this benefit though it is not intended to benefit only them. So, for example, the Sierra Club, an organization that promotes a clean, healthful environment, is considered a public-interest group because the intended beneficiaries of its lobbying include group members and non-group members.

Eight different categories of organizations are involved in the abortion cases examined here, advancing either a pro-choice or a pro-life position. It is useful to distinguish them as public versus private-interest groups since this facilitates a better understanding of the tactics, goals, and restraints of these groups. The "public-interest" camp includes general "public-interest" organizations, civil-liberties groups (public-interest groups that promote civil liberties), religious organizations, nonprofit abortion clinics (not affiliated with Planned Parenthood), women's rights organizations, and legal-aid groups (public-interest organizations that provide pro-bono legal services).

Since the following organizations seek to benefit group members exclusively, included in the private-interest group category are Planned Parenthood and its local affiliates, for-profit abortion clinics not affiliated with Planned Parenthood, professional associations and various types of unions, and a public hospital.

General Public-Interest Groups

Nineteen public-interest groups appeared in the federal-court abortion cases examined here, representing about 11 percent of the total organizational litigants (n = 166). Of these nineteen public-interest groups, eleven (approximately 57 percent) represented the pro-choice side in their litigation efforts.

With regard to overall characteristics of public-interest groups, pro-choice and pro-life, the ideological split in public-interest groups probably impairs their overall success in abortion litigation. In the federal district court cases examined, public-interest groups had a success rate considerably lower than the overall average of 81 percent, prevailing in only 67 percent of the abortion cases in which they became involved (see Appendix D).

Otherwise, public-interest groups tended to be younger than the other types of groups; while the average age for all organizational litigants was thirty-seven years, public-interest groups averaged only twenty-two years of age (in 1992). This suggests that these organizations tend to be relatively new additions to the interest-group system.

Corresponding to their youth, public-interest groups also appeared to be weak organizations in terms of their budgets and staffs. Abortion litigants had average annual budgets of $11 million, while public-interest groups had to fulfill their mandates with average budgets in the amount of $1.1 million. The public-interest groups had staffs that averaged sixteen staff members, while the mean staff for all organizations consisted of 295 members. Of course, it is not surprising that public-interest groups had to augment their limited resources by utilizing volunteers. In fact, 93 percent of the public-interest groups used volunteers versus 86 percent for all organizational litigants. More than 71 percent of the public-interest groups relied upon private donations as their main source of organizational support. Only 21 percent of the public-interest groups indicated that they relied upon membership dues as the primary source of funds, and another 8 percent suggested that the government supplied most of their financial support.

Public-interest groups ranked sixth out of the eleven groups in terms of the frequency with which they became involved in litigation in the federal courts (see Appendix C). While the average score for all organizations on the repeat-player measure, which examines whether the groups were frequently involved in federal court cases, was 23 percent, only 14.3 percent of the public-interest groups indicated that they are repeat players.

These groups also ranked low on the political-activism scale, which measures the involvement of abortion-litigation groups in testifying before Congress on judicial appointments, testifying before Congress on bills generally, financing Congressional campaigns, and meeting with agencies with regard to proposed rules and regulations (see Appendix E). Specifically, public-interest groups fell below the average activism level of 44 percent, with only 35.7 percent of the public-interest groups reporting that they are highly involved in the political process in the United States. Public-interest organizations ranked sixth out of eleven organizational types on this measure.

Public-interest groups fared even more poorly on a "high inter-group cooperation" scale that tests the extent to which groups engage in informal exchanges of information, attend seminars, and engage in joint litigation, ranking ninth out of eleven groups. While the average inter-group cooperation score for all types of groups was 52 percent, only 21.4 percent of the public-interest groups ranked high on the inter-group cooperation measure (see Appendix F).

The only high marks scored by public-interest groups were on the *amicus-curiae* scale, which measures the extent to which groups rely exclusively upon *amicus-curiae* briefs in their federal court litigation efforts (see Appendix G). Public-interest groups ranked second out of nine groups on this measure, with 28.6 percent of the public-interest groups indicating that they file only *amicus* briefs. This contrasts with the overall organizational average: only 17.1 percent of all groups report sole reliance on *amicus-curiae* appearances. This high reliance on *amicus* appearances by public-interest organizations might be the result of their limited resources because participating through *amicus* filings is one way in which to reduce the costs of litigation.

Related to the heavy reliance on *amicus* briefs as a means to minimize litigation costs and maximize efficiency, public-interest groups also were more highly concerned in their litigation efforts with changing legal precedent, as opposed to merely helping litigants or to a combination of the two goals. Public-interest groups ranked third out of nine groups on a policy-oriented litigation scale, with 14.3 percent of the public-interest groups suggesting their sole litigation goal was to change legal precedent, while the overall score for all organizations was 12.5 percent (see Appendix H).

Since this part of the discussion focuses upon pro-choice groups, Table 4.1 (see page 49) lists only the pro-choice public-interest groups that became involved in federal district court cases dealing with abortion during the 1973–1990 period, their inputs to the federal courts, and their overall success rates in litigation.

Pro-choice public-interest groups had a considerably higher success rate in federal court litigation than the broader category of all public-interest groups. Recall that public-interest groups, which includes both pro-choice and pro-life contingents, had a relatively low success rate in litigation, prevailing in only 67 percent of the abortion cases in which they became involved. In contrast, pro-choice public-interest groups won 83 percent of the time.

Pro-choice public-interest groups had greater resources than the overall public-interest-group category. While the average annual budget of public-interest groups was about $1.1 million, pro-choice public-interest groups enjoyed an annual budget in the amount of $2.7 million (n = 7). Pro-choice public-interest groups also had slightly larger staffs, with an average staff size of seventeen people, as opposed to sixteen for all public-interest groups. The pro-choice public-interest groups tended to be older than the overall public-interest groups as well; the average age for pro-choice public-interest groups was thirty-five years, consid-

Table 4.1

Pro-Choice Public Interest Groups' Participation In Abortion Cases

Group	% Wins
Cases	
1. **American Humanist Association** *421 F.Supp. 533* *488 F.Supp. 181* *491 F.Supp. 630*	66%
2. **Americans United for Separation of Church and State** *421 F.Supp. 533* *491 F.Supp. 630*	50%
3. **Chicago Welfare Rights Organization** *469 F.Supp. 1212*	100%
4. **Coalition for Right to Choice, Inc.** *476 F.Supp. 324*	100%
5. **Concern for Health Options: Information, Care and Education, Inc.** *401 F.Supp. 554*	100%
6. **Massachusetts Welfare Recipients for Welfare Reform** *463 F.Supp. 222*	100%
7. **National Abortion Federation** *721 F.Supp. 1168*	0%
8. **National Health Law Program** *383 F.Supp. 1143*	100%
9. **Parents Aid Society, Inc.** *393 F.Supp. 847* *450 F.Supp. 997* *463 F.Supp. 222*	100%
10. **Philadelphia Welfare Rights Organization** *464 F.Supp. 483* *464 F.Supp. 487*	100%
11. **YWCA--Young Women's Christian Association of the U.S.A** *421 F.Supp. 533*	100%

erably older than the twenty-two-year figure for the general public-interest-group category.

Perhaps because of their greater resources, pro-choice public-interest groups did not rely as heavily on the services of volunteers. While 93 percent of the public-interest groups reported using volunteers, only 85 percent of the pro-choice public-interest groups used volunteers.

The two types of groups, general public-interest and pro-choice public-interest, were about tied on the repeat-player measure, which examines whether organizations were frequently involved in federal court litigation. While 14.3 percent of the general public-interest groups classified themselves as repeat players, 14 percent of the pro-choice public-interest groups indicated that they were repeatedly involved in litigation in the federal courts.

However, the two types of groups diverged in terms of their levels of political activism and the extent to which they engaged in inter-group cooperation. Only 35.7 percent of the overall public-interest group fell into the category of political activists—that is, they had above-average involvement in lobbying Congress on judicial appointments, lobbying Congress on bills generally, financing Congressional campaigns, and meeting with agencies with regard to proposed rules and regulations. This contrasts with a political-activism level of 42 percent (n = 7) for the pro-choice public-interest groups.

The pro-choice public-interest groups also benefited from higher levels of inter-group cooperation, which includes such activities as informal exchanges of information, attending seminars, and joint litigation. Some 28 percent of the pro-choice public-interest groups suggested they were highly involved in inter-group cooperation, while the score was only 21.4 percent for the overall public-interest-group category.

One of the pro-choice public-interest groups examined in this analysis is Americans United for Separation of Church and State (Americans United), located in Silver Springs, Maryland. This national organization was founded in 1947. Its operating budget is about $1.4 million, it has a staff of twelve, and it receives most of its funds from individual donors. It ranked quite low in terms of political activism, only infrequently lobbying Congress on bills, and meeting with agencies regarding proposed regulations. It was also only occasionally involved in litigation in the federal courts and interacts with other groups through informal exchanges of information only.

In the federal court abortion cases examined here, Americans United was involved in only two cases and had a success rate of only 50 percent. Perhaps diminishing the group's effectiveness in abortion litigation is the fact that Americans United is primarily concerned with ensuring the separation of church and state in the United States and becomes involved in an abortion case only when this separation is jeopardized. In an organizational pamphlet that seeks to recruit new members, there is no statement of American United's position on the issues of reproductive freedom and abortion (*Americans United 1991*). In fact, nowhere does the pamphlet mention that the organization was involved in abortion litigation in the federal courts and advocated a pro-choice position. Instead, the pamphlet remains intentionally vague, giving no clue to prospective members that some of its organizational resources may have been utilized in this manner.

For example, the pamphlet states:

> Since 1947, Americans United has worked to protect the constitutional principle of church-state separation, a vital cornerstone of religious liberty. Americans of many faiths and political viewpoints, individuals from all walks of life, have come together to defend our freedoms. . . . Mandatory prayer in public schools, tax dollars for parochial schools, government intrusion into religious affairs and meddling in partisan politics by religious groups are among the troubling issues that threaten the protective wall between church and state (*Americans United 1991*: 1).

Once again, there is no specific mention of threats to reproductive freedom and abortion rights as "troubling issues," nor is there any indication that the group has worked to advance these rights.

Even in the discussion of the Americans United's litigation efforts, the pamphlet, probably out of a fear of alienating future members, omits any reference to its abortion-related litigation in the federal courts. The following is, almost in full, the pamphlet's discussion of the group's litigation record:

> Americans United calls on the expertise of the nation's leading church-state lawyers to direct our program of protecting religious freedom rights and church-state separation through court action. . . . We are regularly involved in a large number of court cases, setting legal precedents on behalf of church-state separation. We initiate lawsuits, provide legal counsel and support in other cases, and serve as partners in joint lawsuits. . . . Over the years many of our cases have gone to the U.S. Supreme Court (*Americans United 1991*: 3).

Another pro-choice public-interest group involved in abortion litigation in the federal courts was Concern for Health Options: Information,

Care and Education, Inc., also known as "Choice." It prevailed in the one federal court case it was involved in. The group was founded in 1971, has a staff of thirty-five, relies on volunteers, and operates on an annual budget of $1 million. It is sometimes involved in litigation in the federal courts and is low on the political-activism scale, engaging in lobbying agencies with regard only to proposed rules and regulations.

Choice is dedicated to ensuring that all individuals in the United States have access to quality health and child care, especially persons with low incomes and teens (Choice 1990). According to an information pamphlet:

> The health of our community depends on the ability of people to make informed choices. Choices about reproductive health, AIDS, child care, and other critical issues. Yet for many people, particularly low-income people and teens, the options are limited. That's why Choice was created. By helping people make informed choices, we work to assure access to quality health and child care for all who need it (*Choice 1991*: 1).

Choice carries out this mandate by helping individuals find the health and child care services they need through telephone referrals, educating professionals and the community about these issues, and advocating for better and more accessible services (Choice 1991).

Choice's 1990 annual report goes into considerable detail outlining some of the programs which occupied most of the organization's time and other resources. The report suggests that:

> More than 27,000 women, men and teens turned to the Choice Hotline with questions about birth control, pregnancy, prenatal care, abortion, adoption, sexually transmitted diseases and AIDS. Our highly trained staff provided information, short-term counseling and referrals to help each caller locate the services they needed (*Choice 1990*: 1).

The organization did not, however, overlook the importance of advocacy work; the report continues:

> We wrote a report summarizing the effects of Pennsylvania's 1985 cutoff of abortion funding for medical assistance recipients. . . . Supportive state legislators and the American Civil Liberties Union worked with us

to distribute the report to state politicians and policy makers" (*Choice 1990*: 1).

At a later point, Choice "board and staff went to Harrisburg to meet with Pennsylvania legislators and advocate for additional funding for comprehensive family planning services" (*Choice 1990*: 2). Other activities that occupied Choice staff were making child-care referrals, engaging in training and education programs, and conducting educational theater productions for teens that raised such issues as teen sexuality, drug abuse, and parent/child communication (Choice 1990).

The overall assessment of pro-choice public-interest groups is that they are not really significant players in abortion litigation; at most, they play a secondary role. What damages the effectiveness of public-interest groups as a general group is that there is a huge ideological division between pro-choice and pro-life public-interest groups. But even within the pro-choice contingent, public-interest groups, as Americans United and Choice demonstrate, tend to have organizational goals that diverge as well as very idiosyncratic organizational tasks. Some of the public-interest organizations that advocate a pro-choice position in the federal courts might find it in their best interests to avoid publishing this fact to their members and prospective members. Hence, the contribution of pro-choice public-interest groups to pro-choice abortion litigation in the federal courts is not significant.

Civil-Liberties Groups

Twenty of the 166 pro-choice groups (12 percent) that appeared in post-*Roe v. Wade* abortion cases were civil-liberties groups, or public-interest groups that focus on civil-liberties concerns. Eighteen of these were either the national office of the ACLU or affiliates of the ACLU. Only two were independent of the ACLU: the Center for Constitutional Rights and the Center for Law in the Public Interest (see page 60). Table 4.2 (see pages 54–55) lists the names of each of these pro-choice civil liberties groups, the cases they were involved in, and their overall success rates in litigation.

Once again, all of the civil-liberties groups involved in abortion litigation adopted a pro-choice stance and tended to be quite successful

Table 4.2

Pro-Choice Civil Rights Groups' Participation In Abortion Cases

Group	% Wins
Cases	
1. American Civil Liberties Union	77%
384 F.Supp. 7	
393 F.Supp. 847	
421 F.Supp. 533	
461 F.Supp. 682	
479 F.Supp. 1172	
491 F.Supp. 630	
579 F.Supp. 464	
598 F.Supp. 625	
733 F.Supp. 1036	
2. American Civil Liberties Union Foundation	100%
434 F.Supp. 1048	
489 F.Supp. 238	
550 F.Supp. 1112	
604 F.Supp. 141	
648 F.Supp. 756	
3. American Civil Liberties Union Foundation of Florida	100%
482 F.Supp. 529	
4. American Civil Liberties Union Foundation of San Diego and Imperial Counties	0%
721 F.Supp. 1168	
5. American Civil Liberties Union Foundation of Southern California	0%
721 F.Supp. 1168	
6. American Civil Liberties Union--Ohio	100%
479 F.Supp. 1172	
604 F.Supp. 1268	
604 F.Supp. 1275	
633 F.Supp. 1123	
7. American Civil Liberties Union of Denver	100%
489 F.Supp. 238	
8. American Civil Liberties Union of Georgia	100%
670 F.Supp. 971	
9. American Civil Liberties Union of Louisiana, Inc.	100%
434 F.Supp. 1048	
733 F.Supp. 1036	
10. American Civil Liberties Union of Pennyslvania	100%
464 F.Supp. 483	
464 F.Supp. 487	

Table 4.2 (Cont.)
Pro-Choice Civil Rights Groups' Participation In Abortion Cases

11. **Center for Constitutional Rights**	75%
358 F.Supp. 1193	
409 F.Supp. 731	
421 F.Supp. 533	
491 F.Supp. 630	
12. **Center for Law in the Public Interest**	100%
368 F.Supp. 11	
13. **Connecticut Civil Liberties Union**	100%
482 F.Supp. 725	
14. **Iowa Civil Liberties Union**	100%
361 F.Supp. 1288	
15. **Massachusetts Civil Liberties Union Foundation**	100%
463 F.Supp. 222	
16. **Ohio Civil Liberties Union**	100%
389 F.Supp. 387	
389 F.Supp. 393	
17. **Red River Valley of the ACLU**	100%
497 F.Supp. 1340	
18. **Rhode Island Affiliate ACLU**	100%
358 F.Supp. 1193	
19. **Roger Baldwin Foundation of the ACLU**	89%
448 F.Supp. 997	
449 F.Supp. 1302	
469 F.Supp. 1212	
568 F.Supp. 1490	
579 F.Supp. 377	
579 F.Supp. 464	
584 F.Supp. 1452	
625 F.Supp. 1212	
711 F.Supp. 439	
20. **Wisconsin Civil Liberties Union Foundation**	100%
476 F.Supp. 324	

in terms of judicial decisions. By far the most important player in the civil-liberties camp was the ACLU and its various affiliated groups, including the ACLU Foundation and local ACLU offices throughout the United States. The national office of the ACLU was founded in 1920, and the main office is located in New York City. By 1992 the ACLU had grown to 375,000 members, a staff of 120, and a budget of more than $12 million. The ACLU employs volunteers extensively and has 50 state groups and more than 200 local groups. The major sources of funds for the ACLU are membership dues and private donations. The goal of the ACLU is to defend the freedoms guaranteed under the Constitution and, specifically, the Bill of Rights.

The enormous resources available to the ACLU and the ACLU Foundation enable the organization to divide itself into different specialized units; for example, special units of the national office work on prisoners' rights and gay rights. Similarly, to protect reproductive rights, the ACLU established the Reproductive Freedom Project. According to the Reproductive Freedom Project's 1990 annual report:

> the goal of the Reproductive Freedom Project is to protect the constitutional right to privacy—particularly in the area of reproductive choice—including the right to choose between childbirth and abortion; the right to obtain and use contraceptives regardless of age; and the right to choose between sterilization and fertility (*ACLU 1990*: ix).

The project pursues its goal of protecting reproductive choice through a variety of methods, including public-education campaigns; legislative lobbying; litigation aimed at blocking the implementation of restrictive federal, state, and local laws; and federal agency actions that restrict access to this right (ACLU 1990).

In a 1992 survey, a representative of the national ACLU admitted that the organization is frequently involved in federal court litigation, sometimes lobbies Congress on judicial appointments, frequently testifies before Congress on bills, and sometimes meets with agencies regarding proposed rules and regulations.

The Reproductive Freedom Project engages in an impressive array of activities, such as sponsoring major cases dealing with reproductive-freedom rights before the Supreme Court, becoming involved in state constitutional cases in which these same rights are challenged, and providing to litigants and other organizations invaluable support during litigation. With regard to the latter, the project maintains and publishes a docket summarizing the status of all cases dealing with reproductive freedom that are currently pending in United States courts. Project staff also are regularly consulted by lawyers and organizations involved in reproductive-freedom cases. Project staff may review and edit complaints, briefs, and other litigation papers; provide factual information; and advise on strategy for briefing and oral argument (ACLU 1990).

Aside from litigation-related activities, the ACLU, as mentioned earlier, is actively involved in lobbying executive- and legislative-branch officials with regard to national policies on reproductive-freedom rights, including abortion. As explained in a 1990 report:

"Because the fundamental right to choose is more vulnerable to the political process in the wake of *Webster* than at any time since 1973, the ACLU Foundation has devoted substantial resources for public outreach and critical technical assistance to the many local pro-choice coalitions and activists" (*ACLU 1990*: 26). The report suggests that a key player is the Reproductive Freedom Project's State Coordinating Counsel, Kathryn Kolbert, who lobbied at the state level for fourteen years and is an experienced litigator. It continues: "Monitoring activities around the country, Ms. Kolbert developed model briefing papers, model legislation, in-depth fact sheets and analyses, and developed grassroots strategies to counter attacks on women's rights to choose" (*ACLU 1990*: 26). The unique advantage of the ACLU over other organizations involved in abortion litigation is that it is one of the few pro-choice groups with an affiliate or chapter in every state. According to the report, as a result of this, "the Project was able to provide accurate and up-to-date information about state-level assaults on reproductive freedom to the press, policy makers, and legislators" (*ACLU 1990*: 26).

The coalition-building activities of the ACLU's Reproductive Freedom Project provide striking testimony to the strength of the pro-choice lobby in the United States. The 1990 report also states:

> During 1990, more than 400 anti-choice bills were introduced into the 44 state legislatures that were in session. In at least 40 of these states, Project staff provided assistance and support to activists countering anti-choice efforts, which included: outright bans on abortion, bans on abortion for "sex selection," mandatory delays and forced doctor lectures, parental notification and consent provisions, husband notification, clinic inspection and staff reporting requirements, compulsory viability testing, restrictions on post 24-week abortions, bans on fetal tissue research and experimentation, feticide statutes, penalties against pregnant women who use drugs, and restrictions on public funding for abortion and birth control. Significant battles were fought in numerous states. . . . In each instance, the Project, in consultation with ACLU state affiliates, played a leading role in analyzing the measures and providing strategic support (*ACLU 1990*: 26–27).

The coalition activities of the ACLU's Reproductive Freedom Project not only operated within the ACLU and its affiliates, but also extended to external groups. Project staff regularly consulted with other national groups about state-level activities and provided legal expertise to pro-choice-coalition partners. According to the report: "Regularly sharing information and strategy helped the pro-choice groups be more effective and efficient, and enabled us to spot problems and improve strategy at the local level" (*ACLU 1990*: 27).

In the summer of 1990, the project organized a unique evaluative conference in Washington, DC. The report states:

> to evaluate our state-level efforts and develop plans for the coming year, the Project organized a State Strategy Training Conference. . . . Bringing together ACLU staff working on issues of reproductive freedom on both the state and federal level, the conference developed greater expertise within our local affiliates, disseminated the knowledge gleaned from our state-level activity, and strengthened the national network of pro-choice activists (*ACLU 1990*: 27).

In addition to coalition building, the Reproductive Freedom Project has also undertaken a State Constitution Project in which ACLU activists seek state constitutional change to promote full reproductive freedom. The reason for the new emphasis on state constitutions is the insecurity shared by many ACLU members that the United States Supreme Court will overturn or seriously undermine federal constitutional protection for a woman's right to choose. According to the report:

> The first victory for the State Constitution Project came in 1989, when the Florida Supreme court struck down the state's parental consent requirement, finding that the Florida Constitution accords greater protection to privacy rights than the federal Constitution. . . . In 1990, the Project helped the ACLU of California challenge the state's parental involvement statute, hoping to capitalize on an earlier ruling by the California judiciary that rejected the exclusion of abortion from the state's Medicaid program on state constitutional grounds (*ACLU 1990*: 28).

Because of the undeniable link between resources and political efficacy, in 1990 the Project launched a program of providing small grants to under-funded ACLU state affiliates (ACLU 1990). Specifically, grants have gone to ACLU affiliates in Alabama, Colorado, Idaho, Louisiana, Mississippi, and Oregon. Through these grants, the project hopes to generate broad grassroots support for the project and the ACLU.

The ACLU of Northern California (ACLUNC) is one of the local affiliates of the ACLU that pushes for statewide reforms through a broad strategy of litigation, lobbying, and advocacy. In its publication, ACLUNC notes: "We have come to believe that we can often achieve better results for less outside of court. This means that we think of direct advocacy as a primary tool, not just as an alternative when litigation is unattractive" (*ACLUNC 1990*: 1).

The primary objective for ACLUNC in 1990 was to protect the state constitutional right to privacy as an independent source of support for reproductive choice. Margaret Crosby, a staff attorney for ACLUNC, played a critical role in statewide coalition-building. In addition to her ACLU activities, she served as a legal consultant to the California Coalition for Reproductive Freedom, a statewide coalition of pro-choice organizations. In this capacity, Crosby had many speaking engagements and media appearances, and wrote extensively on the subject of reproductive freedom.

Of course, the local ACLU organization also engaged in litigation. According to its report: "In our own case concerning young women's access to abortion (*American Academy of Pediatrics v. Van de Kamp*), the California Court of Appeal issued a strong ruling reaffirming the independence of California's right to privacy and refusing to permit enforcement of a law restricting abortion" (*ACLUNC 1990*: 3).

In another case in which ACLUNC was involved, the State Court of Appeal upheld a lower court order in 1989, enjoining the enforcement of California's 1987 law requiring teenagers to obtain parental consent or a court order before they can have an abortion. This earlier case originated in 1987 after the law in question was passed by the state legislature and signed by the governor. The suit was filed by ACLUNC and the Adolescent Health Care Project of the National Center for Youth, and then joined by a coalition of medical organizations and health-care providers. According to the ACLUNC report: "The plaintiffs submitted extensive expert testimony on teenagers' capacity to make informed decisions about pregnancy and about the devastating impact parental involvement laws have on young women's health" (*ACLUNC 1990*: 3).

Of course, ACLUNC also spent considerable time and energy on extra-judicial lobbying. For example, the organization in its 1990 report takes credit for the fact that the state legislature, for the first time since 1978, did not place restrictions on Medi-Cal funds for abortions in 1989. The report claims:

> This victory resulted in part because of extensive lobbying efforts by our legislative advocates, activists, and members. For the past twelve years, Medi-Cal funds for abortions were provided only because of the successful legal challenges brought by the ACLU-NC on behalf of a coalition of Medi-Cal recipients, abortion providers, women's and welfare rights organizations (*ACLUNC 1990*: 3).

As mentioned earlier, only two of the twenty civil-liberties groups are independent of the ACLU: the Center for Law in the Public Interest, located in Los Angeles, California, and the Center for Constitutional Rights, based in New York City. An interview was completed only for the New York organization. The Center for Constitutional Rights was founded in 1966, has a staff of twenty-four, and has a budget of $1.8 million, derived mostly from private foundations and individual donors. The group is frequently involved in litigation in the federal courts, including abortion cases. However, it also is politically active in that it engages in advocacy work, testifies before Congress on judicial appointments, meets with agencies regarding proposed rules and regulations, and testifies before Congress generally. When it cooperates with other groups, it is usually through joint litigation.

What is striking about civil-liberties groups is that they are all prochoice and tend to receive preferential court rulings when involved in post-*Roe v. Wade* (1973) abortion litigation (Supra, Chapter 2). While the average success rate for groups was 81 percent, civil-liberties groups enjoyed a success rate of 87 percent, ranking second on a litigation-success scale (see Appendix D).

Civil-liberties groups are usually small organizations in comparison to other groups involved in abortion cases. While the average annual budget of all groups was $11 million, civil-liberties groups averaged only $2.4 million. The staffs of civil-liberties groups also averaged only 21 in number, while the group average was 295 staff members.

Civil-liberties groups derive most of their support from private donations: 79 percent of the groups listed this as a primary source of funds, while only 21 percent responded that membership dues are a main source of organizational support. Not a single civil-liberties groups listed the government, fees, or grants as major sources of support.

With respect to the organizational advantage of longevity, the mean age of thirty-nine for civil-liberties groups fell very close to the overall mean of thirty-seven years.

One way in which the civil-liberties groups were distinguished from other organizations involved in abortion litigation is in their extensive use of volunteers. Only 86 percent of all of the other organizations used volunteers, while fully 100 percent of the civil-liberties organizations use volunteers extensively, regularly incorporating them into important organizational tasks.

Civil-liberties groups also far surpassed other groups in the extent to which they involve themselves in the political process. While 44 percent of all groups engaged in abortion litigation are highly involved in the political process, 73.7 percent (or seventeen of the twenty civil-liberties groups) are active participants in politics in the United States. They ranked second of eleven groups on a political-activism scale (see Appendix E). The political activities of these civil-liberties groups include: testifying before Congress on judicial appointments, testifying before Congress on bills generally, financing Congressional campaigns, and meeting with agencies with regard to proposed rules and regulations.

Political activism is carried on by civil-liberties groups at both the national and local level, with some division of responsibility taking place. The national office of the ACLU, for example, focuses its energies on federal-level lobbying, while affiliates of the ACLU concentrate on state and local policies that impair reproductive-freedom rights, though there is some overlap in these activities. The efforts of civil-liberties groups to have an impact on public policies are often quite productive.

The civil-liberties groups, through their political lobbying and publicity campaigns, acquire an important litigation resource: visibility. This, perhaps, helps serve to explain the preferential court decisions these groups received in post-*Roe v. Wade* abortion litigation. In their litigation efforts, civil-liberties groups tend to utilize an offensive litigation strategy, appearing typically as the petitioner for relief in court cases. Other ideologically similar groups often lend their assistance to these cases. The relief civil-liberties groups seek is to undo national, state, and local policies that obstruct reproductive-freedom rights.

Although the twenty civil-liberties groups included in this analysis represented only 12 percent of the groups that became involved in abortion litigation, they were involved in 44 of the 145 total cases, or 33 percent of the total. Not surprisingly, civil-liberties groups scored highest of all groups on the repeat-player measure, with fourteen out of nineteen, or 74 percent of the civil-liberties groups indicating they are frequently involved in litigation (see Appendix C). Civil-liberties groups also ranked highest of all groups on the inter-group cooperation measure, with 79 percent of the total engaged in a high level of inter-group cooperation, including informal exchanges of information, attending seminars, and engaging in joint litigation (see Appendix F).

Nevertheless, the statistical analysis engaged in Chapter 2 indicates that the fact that a group is a civil-liberties group is a significant predictor of litigation success, even when one controls for the repeat-player status of the group and whether the group engaged in high levels of inter-group cooperation. As such, the success of civil-liberties groups in litigation is not a result of their repeat-player status or their cooperation with other, similar groups. Instead, their success is probably linked to their high visibility and their popularity with members of the federal bench.

Religious Groups

Although religious organizations are usually associated with the pro-life position, a rather surprising finding is that most of the religious organizations involved in post-*Roe v. Wade* abortion litigation adopted a pro-choice position in these cases. The eighteen religious groups involved in these cases constituted 11 percent of the 166 groups present. Sixteen of the religious groups, or 89 percent, sided with a pro-choice position. For this reason, I have included them here. What follows, then, is general discussion of religious groups, although those individual pro-choice religious groups are also to be addressed when the discussion focuses upon pro-choice religious groups.

Overall, religious organizations, whether they adopted a pro-choice or pro-life position, were not at an advantage in the abortion cases examined here. While the average success rate for all groups was 81 percent, religious organizations had an overall success rate far below the mean, prevailing in only 52 percent of the cases. They ranked tenth of eleven groups on a litigation success scale (see Appendix D). Further, when one controls for other variables, it was earlier found that religious groups do not have the upper hand in litigation (Chapter 2). The fact that a group is a religious group increases its probability of prevailing in abortion litigation by only 5.5 percent, which is not statistically significant ($t = .27$, $p = .79$).

The mean age for all organizational litigants was thirty-seven years (in 1992). The mean age for religious organizations was considerably higher, at fifty-seven years. The average 268-member staff size of religious groups is somewhat lower than the organizational norm of 295. Also falling slightly below the mean budget of $11 million, religious groups have a mean budget of about $8.15 million. However, 100 percent of the religious organizations use volunteers, which is considerably higher than the overall mean of 86 percent. So, in terms of overall organizational resources, religious groups are not very distinct from most organizations involved in abortion litigation.

Religious groups engaged in a lower level of inter-group cooperation than the overall average; these groups ranked eighth out of eleven types of organizations on the "high inter-group cooperation" measure, which assesses the extent to which organizational litigants exchange information with each other on an informal level (such as through sporadic telephone calls), send their representatives to conferences attended by the agents of other groups, and engage in joint litigation (see Appendix F).

Out of 166 post-*Roe* abortion cases, the eighteen religious groups, which comprise 11 percent of all organizational litigants, collectively made twenty-five inputs to the courts, for a total organizational involvement of 13 percent. However, this figure, by itself, is somewhat misleading. Some of the religious groups often banded together, becoming involved as *amicus curiae* or litigants in just a few major cases. Nevertheless, collectively, religious groups were second in rank on a repeat-player measure (whether the organization is frequently involved in federal court litigation). While the mean on the repeat-player variable was 23 percent, religious groups scored second in rank, behind civil-liberties groups. Specifically, in response to a question of whether they are frequently involved in federal-court litigation, 73.7 percent of the civil-liberties groups responded affirmatively, followed by religious groups at 29.4 percent (see Appendix C).

The repeat-player status of religious groups did not lead to success in litigation; as noted earlier, religious groups tended to have success rates far lower than average in post-*Roe* abortion litigation in the federal courts (see Appendix D). Similarly, religious groups ranked rather high—fourth out of twelve—relative to all groups on a political-activism scale, which measures the extent to which a group engages in extra-judicial lobbying, including: testifying before Congress on bills, testifying before Congress on bills generally, financing Congressional campaigns, and meeting with agency officials with regard to proposed rules and regulations (see Appendix E). As such, religious organizations should also be assisted in their litigation efforts by their relatively high level of visibility. Other organizations that have a high level of visibility, such as the civil-liberties groups discussed earlier in this chapter, seem to be aided in their litigation efforts by it.

Three major factors account, however, for the higher success level enjoyed by civil-liberties groups in federal court litigation. First, as noted earlier, the religious groups that appeared in federal court cases, unlike the uniformly pro-choice civil-liberties groups, fell into two different ideological camps: pro-choice and pro-life. As a result, religious groups did not send a clear message to federal judges in their litigation efforts. Second, civil-liberties groups, because of their unbiased commitment to civil rights, speak with greater moral authority than religious groups, which, like all organizations, seek to ensure organizational security and growth.

Another explanation for the higher success rate of civil-liberties groups in abortion litigation is that federal court judges do not want to be perceived as siding with one religious group over another in court cases. These comments are even more relevant when the cases that judges preside over, as is true with the abortion cases here, give rise to an explosive and ideological public debate. As such, the low success rate of religious groups in abortion cases is not altogether surprising. District court judges apparently chose to steer a nonconfrontational path when dealing with religious-organization litigants in not giving full weight, to the preferences (or "legal arguments") of religious groups in their final decisions.

One of the pro-choice religious organizations that appeared in the federal court cases examined here was Catholics for a Free Choice (CHOICE), a national organization whose headquarters are in Washington, DC. The organization was founded in 1973, has a full-time staff of eleven, and has an operating budget of $800,000, most of which is derived from foundation grants and individual donors. CHOICE employs volunteers extensively in its day-to-day operations. The aggregate picture, then, is of a relatively small organization.

The group sometimes engages in federal court litigation, sometimes lobbies Congress on judicial appointments, sometimes testifies before Congress on bills, never finances Congressional campaigns, and sometimes meets with agencies regarding proposed rules and regulations. The primary litigation strategy of the organization is to file *amicus-curiae* briefs in pending court cases. The organization was involved in only two of the cases included in this analysis, and its success rate was quite low at 50 percent. The two cases are *McRae v. Mathews*, 421 F. Supp. 533 (1976), in which the lower court found that the federal ban on Medicaid for elective abortions violates *Roe v. Wade*, and *McRae v. Califano*, (1980) 491 F. Supp. 630, in which the lower court upheld withholding of federal funds for elective abortions.

The organization publishes a newsletter that contains the articles and letters of numerous contributors, all of whom attempt to shed light on the issue of reproductive freedom. CHOICE is dedicated to policy change in the United States which would enhance the reproductive freedom of women. As stated in its newsletter:

> Catholics for a Free Choice (CFFC) is a national educational organization that supports the right to legal reproductive health care, especially family planning and abortion. CFFC also works to reduce the incidence of abortion and to increase women's choices in childbearing and child-rearing through advocacy of social and economic programs for women, families, and children (*Choice 1991*: 2).

Through its involvement in federal court cases that implicate reproductive-freedom rights and extra-judicial public-education campaigns and advocacy efforts, CHOICE is clearly dedicated to causing changes in public policy.

Appearing in the same two court cases with CHOICE (*McRae v. Mathews*, 421 F. Supp. 533 (1976) and *McRae v. Califano*, 491 F. Supp. 630 (1980); (see Appendix B) was another pro-choice religious group, the National Federation of Temple Sisterhoods (NFTS). NFTS is a much older organization than CHOICE, having formed in 1912. It is a national organization whose headquarters are in New York City. It has 125,000 members, a staff of twelve, relies on volunteers, and derives its budget of approximately $1 million from private donations and membership dues. NFTS also pursues an *amicus-curiae* litigation strategy, with the intention of changing legal precedent. Unfortunately, in the two federal district court cases discussed, it also shared CHOICE's poor success rate of 50 percent. NFTS is not frequently involved in federal court litigation, but it sometimes becomes involved in federal court cases.

The position of NFTS on reproductive freedom roughly parallels that of CHOICE. In a 1991 resolution on the general topic of women's health care, NFTS notes that "women are in danger of losing their rights to reproductive health care," (*NFTS 1991*: 19) and called for members to "reaffirm their support for continued funding for and unrestricted access to reproductive services and advice" (*NFTS 1991*: 20).

The organization also engages in extra-judicial lobbying, including lobbying Congress on judicial appointments, testifying before Congress on bills, and meeting with agencies with regard to rules and regulations. NFTS is highly involved in interactions with other organizations via informal exchanges of information, attending seminars, and joint litigation.

A third religious pro-choice group identified in the analysis is the Women's Division of the Board of Global Ministries of the United Methodist Church (hereinafter, the "Women's Division"). The Women's Division was founded in 1940, has its headquarters in New York City, has a staff of forty, relies on volunteers, and had a 1992 budget of $20 million, derived from membership dues.

Political activism by the Women's Division takes the form of lobbying Congress on judicial appointments, testifying before Congress on bills, and meeting with agencies regarding proposed rules and regulations. It engages in only a minimal amount of inter-group cooperation, becoming involved in informal exchanges of information with other similar organizations, but nothing beyond this.

The leadership of the Women's Division is unambiguously committed to preserving reproductive-freedom rights. The position of the Women's Division was set forth in an official publication of the organization in 1975, which has not been altered to date. It states:

Birth control, sex education and abortion rights have never been easy issues for the church, particularly in those denominations where women have no voice in policy-making. The Women's Division has viewed abortion as a significant issue of ministry to women, children and family life. Its relationship to health care, economic realities and ethical decision making has been highlighted. Of paramount concern is a woman's role in those decisions which impact her life in its totality. This perspective is consistent with the United Methodist position detailed in the statement on "Responsible Parenthood". . . . This position is also stated in the 1980 Social Principles which says, in part: "We (the church) support the legal option of abortion under proper medical procedures." (*Women's Division 1975*: S-19).

The Women's Division only infrequently becomes involved in federal court litigation and tends to appear in an *amicus-curiae* role when involved in abortion litigation. The Women's Division also has a poor record in litigation, having lost the only case in which it participated. This case was the by now familiar *McRae v. Califano*, 491 F. Supp. 630 (1980), also joined in by the two other religious pro-choice groups already discussed, NFTS and CHOICE. Barbara Campbell of the Women's Division discusses how the group came to be involved in this case:

In keeping with total church policies, the Women's Division has been active in the Religious Coalition for Abortion Rights, a national organization with some state counterparts. In 1977, the Division took an unprecedented action and joined the case of *McRae v. Harris* (Califano) as plaintiff intervenor in support of the claim of a Medicaid recipient, Mrs. Cora McRae. This case was a class action suit to challenge and overturn federal legislation which denied Medicaid funds for abortion. The position of the Women's Division and others was upheld by the Federal District Court in New York. In 1980, the decision was overturned by the U.S. Supreme Court when it was appealed. The religious and ethical issues put forth by the Women's Division were never discussed or decided by the Supreme Court (*Women's Division 1975*: S-19).

The preceding discussion of the role of the three pro-choice religious groups in abortion litigation suggests that, in spite of their claims, these three groups may have been only peripheral players in these cases. In both *McRae v. Mathews* and *McRae v. Califano*, the religious organizations filed *amicus* briefs in pending cases, lending their "moral support" to the plaintiffs but not playing a key role in defining legal issues, filing cases, and searching for test cases. One suspects that this may be a pattern with respect to (especially pro-choice) religious groups engaged in abortion litigation in the federal courts.

To test whether this is, in fact, an accurate portrayal of the litigation pattern of religious groups in these cases, it is necessary to examine the litigation strategies of religious organizations. In fact, if you examine Appendix G, you will find that religious groups rank first before all other groups in the extent to which they rely solely on the litigation strategy of filing *amicus-curiae* briefs (as opposed to either appearing in a representative capacity or using a combination of the two strategies); 70.6 percent of all religious groups utilize the *amicus-curiae* brief as a sole means of involvement in federal court cases. Public-interest groups were second in rank on this measure, and their exclusive use of *amicus* briefs falls to 28.6 percent; in other words, only 28.6 percent of all public-interest groups exclusively use *amicus* briefs in their litigation efforts.

The assumption here is that organizations that rely to a great extent on *amicus* briefs in their litigation efforts tend to play a passive role in litigation. Consequently, these groups lack control over most of the important aspects of a case, such as the legal and factual issues of the case and deciding upon the proper litigants and judicial forum.

A substantive review of the cases that religious groups were involved in might help with determining whether their participation in litigation was only peripheral, as suggested, or substantial. Once again, eighteen groups are present. Table 4.3 (see page 69) provides the name of each group, whether they are pro-choice or pro-life, the federal court cases they were involved in during the 1973–1990 period, whether they merely filed an *amicus* brief or were more directly involved in litigation efforts, and their overall success rates in litigation.

Undoubtedly, one is again surprised by the fact the religious organizations that appeared in these cases overwhelmingly advocated a pro-choice position. Even more significant is the fact that religious groups played practically no substantive role in these cases. A cursory review of the table reveals that all of the religious groups were involved in only four, or 2 percent of the abortion cases (421 F. Supp. 533, 491 F.

Table 4.3

Religious Groups' Participation In Abortion Cases

Group	Pro-Choice/ Pro-Life	% Wins
Cases	*Amicus/Direct*	
1. American Ethical Union	Choice	50%
421 F.Supp. 533 /491 F.Supp. 630	*amicus*	
2. American Jewish Congress	Choice	0%
491 F.Supp. 630	*amicus*	
3. Board of Church and Society--United Methodist Church	Choice	50%
421 F.Supp. 533/491 F.Supp. 630	*amicus*	
4. Catholics for a Free Choice	Choice	50%
421 F.Supp. 533; 491 F.Supp. 630	*amicus*	
5. Catholic League for Religious and Civil Rights	Life	100%
491 F.Supp. 630	*direct & amicus*	
6. Christian Church (Disciples of Christ)	Choice	0%
491 F.Supp. 630	*amicus*	
7. Christians In Action	Life	100%
681 F.Supp. 688	*direct*	
8. Church of the Brethren	Choice	50%
421 F.Supp. 533/491 F.Supp. 630	*amicus*	
9. National Federation of Temple Sisterhoods	Choice	50%
421 F.Supp. 533/491 F.Supp. 630	*amicus*	
10. National Ministries/American Baptist Churches	Choice	100%
421 F.Supp. 533	*amicus*	
11. National Women's Conference of the American Ethical Union	Choice	100%
421 F.Supp. 533	*amicus*	
12. Office for Church in Society --United Chruch of Christ	Choice	100%
421 F.Supp. 533	*amicus*	
13. Religious Coalition for Abortion Rights	Choice	100%
476 F.Supp. 324	*amicus*	
14. Union of American Hebrew Congregations	Choice	50%
421 F.Supp. 533/491 F.Supp. 630	*amicus*	
15. Unitarian Universalist Women's Federation	Choice	50%
421 F.Supp. 533/491 F.Supp. 630	*amicus*	
16. United Presbyterian Church	Choice	0%
491 F.Supp. 630	*amicus*	
17. United Synagogue of America	Choice	0%
491 F.Supp. 630	*amicus*	
18. Women's Division of the Board of Global Ministries of the United Methodist Church	Choice	0%
491 F.Supp. 630	*amicus*	

Supp. 630, 681 F. Supp. 688, and 476 F. Supp. 324). Further, the pro-choice religious groups, for the most part, appeared in an *amicus* capacity, while other major groups, such as the ACLU and Planned Parenthood, took the dominant role in litigation in the federal courts. A perfect example is the case of *McRae v. Mathews*, 421 F. Supp. 533 (1976), in which the following organizations appeared representing the pro-choice side (there were no organizations representing the pro-life position):

1. Planned Parenthood
2. ACLU
3. Center for Constitutional Rights
4. New York City Health and Hospitals Corporation
5. National Medical Association
6. National Association of Social Workers
7. American Public Health Association
8. NOW
9. American Ethical Union
10. American Humanist Association
11. YWCA
12. Americans United for Separation of Church and State
13. Board of Church and Society—United Methodist Church
14. CHOICE
15. Church of the Brethren
16. NFTS
17. National Ministries—American Baptist Churches in the United States of America
18. National Women's Conference of the American Ethical Union
19. Office for Church in Society—United Church of Christ
20. Union of American Hebrew Congregations
21. Unitarian Universalist Women's Federation.

This suggests that another reason why civil-liberties groups have more success than pro-choice religious groups in federal court litigation in abortion cases is because religious groups are only passive litigators, filing *amicus-curiae* briefs in cases that are already pending. These briefs are filed not because of the strength of the legal arguments they present—this task is far better performed by expert, specialist legal counsel provided by, for example, civil-liberties groups and Planned

Parenthood—but primarily to show that the religious community in the United States does not speak with a unified voice on the abortion issue. This lack of unity leaves federal court judges free of pressure from organized religion. Instead, judges may then dwell upon the arguments presented by the major players in litigation, including civil-liberties groups.

Women's Rights Groups

Women's organizations tend to be smaller and less well-funded than other organizational litigants. The mean budget for all groups in 1992 was $11 million, while women's groups averaged only about $2 million. Their staff size was also below the overall average of 295; women's groups had small staffs, with an average of only eighteen staff members. Not surprisingly, 100 percent of the women's groups use volunteers in their operations. The women's groups were also somewhat younger than other types of groups: the average age for women's groups in 1992 was thirty-one years, while the overall average was thirty-seven years.

It is somewhat surprising that women's groups were not major players in the abortion cases examined here. Only nine, or roughly 5 percent, of the total organizational presence consisted of women's groups. All of the women's organizations were aligned with the pro-choice position. The identity of these nine groups, the cases they became involved in, whether they are pro-choice or pro-life, their litigation strategies, and their success rates are all contained in Table 4.4 (see page 72).

Overall, the women's groups were rather successful in abortion litigation in the federal courts, prevailing in 86 percent of the cases, which is considerably higher than the overall average of 81 percent (see Appendix D). These nine women's rights organizations, or 5 percent of the total, were involved in 10 of the 145 total abortion cases, or only about 6 percent of the cases. Clearly, then, women's groups comprise a small percentage of the organizational litigants, and those present were not active litigators in the federal court abortion cases examined. Accordingly, the groups ranked themselves quite poorly on a repeat-player measure: only 20 percent of the women's rights organizations indicated that they make frequent forays into the federal courts. While the overall average was 23 percent, women's groups ranked fifth out of eleven groups on this measure (see Appendix C).

Table 4.4

Women's Groups' Participation In Abortion Cases

Group	Pro-Choice/ Pro Life	%Wins
Cases	*Amicus/Direct*	
1. **Fifty-First State National Organization for Women**	Choice	100%
726 F.Supp. 1483	*Direct*	
	(filed case)	
2. **Georgia National Organization for Women**	Choice	100%
670 F.Supp. 971	*Direct*	
3. **League of Women Voters**	Choice	100%
670 F.Supp. 971	*Amicus*	
4. **Maryland National Organization for Women**	Choice	100%
726 F.Supp. 1483	*Direct*	
5. **National Organization for Women**	Choice	100%
421 F. Supp. 533	*Amicus*	
426 F. Supp. 331	*Direct*	
726 F.Supp. 1483	*Direct*	
	(filed case)	
6. **National Organization for Women, Legal Defense & Education Fund**	Choice	0%
491 F.Supp. 630	*Direct*	
7. **National Organization for Women, Northwest Wayne County Chapter**	Choice	100%
426 F.Supp. 471	*Direct*	
8. **Virginia National Organization for Women**	Choice	100%
726 F.Supp. 1483	*Direct*	
	(filed case)	
9. **Women's Law Project**	Choice	75%
464 F.Supp. 483	*Direct*	
464 F.Supp. 487	*Direct*	
552 F.Supp. 791	*Direct*	
613 F.Supp. 656	*Direct*	

In contrast, women's groups ranked quite highly on the political-activism scale. The political-activism scale measures the extent to which groups engage in one of more of the following activities: testifying before Congress on judicial appointments, testifying before Congress generally, financing Congressional campaigns, and meeting with agencies with regard to proposed rules and regulations. Of the eleven different types of groups, 80 percent of the women's groups reported high levels of involvement in political lobbying. Note that the organizational mean was considerably lower at 44 percent (see Appendix E).

In spite of this, women's groups, as discussed earlier (Chapter 2), were not favored in federal court litigation (to a statistically significant degree).

Women's groups also had high scores on the inter-group cooperation measure, which assesses the extent to which groups engage in informal exchanges of information, send their representatives to conferences attended by other groups, and engage in joint litigation. Women's groups ranked third out of eleven on this scale, with 60 percent of the women's groups engaging in high levels of inter-group cooperation; the overall average was 52 percent (see Appendix F).

Women's groups were somewhat higher than the overall average in their use of *amicus-curiae* briefs as a sole means of engaging in litigation in the federal courts. While 17.1 percent of all groups indicated sole reliance on *amicus* briefs, 20 percent of the women's organizations reported that they engage in litigation solely by filing *amicus curiae* briefs (see Appendix G).

Related to this is that women's groups tended to be more policy-oriented in their federal court abortion-litigation efforts than most of the other types of organizations. About 12.5 percent of all groups claimed that their sole purpose in engaging in abortion litigation is to change legal precedent, rather than to help a litigant. On the other hand, about 20 percent of the women's groups reported that their only concern is to change judicial policy (see Appendix H). In fact, women's groups ranked second of nine groups on this measure, falling behind only religious groups, 41.2 percent of which were solely policy-oriented.

Seven out of the nine women's groups involved in the abortion cases were associated with NOW. The objectives of NOW and its local affiliates are set forth in a pamphlet circulated by the Michigan Conference of NOW:

The purpose of the National Organization for Women is "to take action to bring women into full participation in the mainstream of American society now, exercising all privileges and responsibilities thereof in truly equal partnership with men." NOW seeks to eliminate the roots of sexism in society by actions including lobbying, educating and mobilizing the community on women's rights issues. NOW endorses political candidates who support NOW's stated purpose (*Michigan NOW*: 1991).

Similarly, the 1990 Annual Report of NOW's Legal Defense and Education Fund (LDEF), suggests that after making decades of progress in terms of the elimination of sex-stereotypes, women's rights are currently threatened. Specifically:

The first threat is to the concept of individual autonomy or control of one's bodily integrity. Reproductive health and some of the most important decisions a woman will make in her lifetime—are now more threatened by governmental restriction and intervention than at any time since the turn of the century. The second threat is to the newly created spheres of women's endeavors in society. What will a new society, where men and women are on an equal social, political and economic footing, look like? Winning entry into a male-dominated world is only half the battle—and the less important half at that. The real goal is to help re-make a world that is "user-friendly" for women. That means fighting for childcare and family leave, health programs and decent education of our children, sex equity and freedom from domestic violence. It means fighting to end discrimination based on being differently abled, or one's race, nationality, or sexual orientation, in addition to gender-based discrimination (*NOW 1990*: i).

NOW was founded in 1966, has a staff of thirty, relies to a great extent on volunteers, and had a budget in 1992 of more than $8 million. It is frequently involved in lobbying Congress on judicial appointments and frequently contributes money to congressional campaigns. It becomes involved to a lesser extent in federal court litigation and lobbying Congress on bills generally. The national office is located in Washington, DC, and it engages in a high level of inter-group cooperation. NOW is organized on national, regional, state, and local levels.

In contrast, NOW's LDEF is a younger organization, founded in 1970, with a staff of twenty-five, extensive use of volunteers, and a budget of $1 million. As the legal arm of NOW, it is frequently involved in federal court litigation. To a lesser degree, it also lobbies Congress on judicial appointments, testifies before Congress on bills, and meets with agencies regarding regulations. It engages in high levels of inter-group cooperation.

However, even LDEF engages in advocacy work, and its litigation efforts are the product of a well-designed strategy to have an impact on judicial policy-making. As the 1990 Report suggests,

Since the *Webster* decision represents a serious setback in the courts, our Legal Program has expanded reproductive rights work to include more advocacy, education and technical training, and technical assistance for federal and state legislative work. NOW LDEF published and distributed *Facts On Reproductive Rights: A Resource Manual*—a comprehensive manual on reproductive rights issues (*NOW 1990*: 9).

Still, the organization makes frequent forays into the federal courts to protect reproductive rights, as is shown by the discussion in the LDEF's 1990 Report of "docket highlights" during 1988–1990 in the area of reproductive rights:

NOW v. Operation Rescue (D.C.) Co-counsel for plaintiff . . . We won an injunction protecting women's constitutional rights to travel and privacy against efforts by Operation Rescue extremists to deprive women of those rights by blocking access to women's clinics (similar cases won by NOW LDEF in New York City, Maryland, and Virginia). . . . *In re A.C.* Counsel for amici: . . . The Court of Appeals for the District of Columbia ruled that a pregnant woman, even one who is terminally ill and whose fetus is probably viable, may not be forced against her will to undergo a cesarian delivery as was done in the case of A. C., who died shortly thereafter, as did the fetus. . . . *Webster v. Reproductive Health Service* Counsel for amici: . . . in this landmark case challenging reproductive choice, NOW LDEF filed its own poignant and compelling brief in the U.S. Supreme Court, "Women's Voices." The "Voices" brief documented the first-hand accounts of over 2,000 women and their friends with the experience of reproductive choicemaking, abortion and birth control [pre- and post-*Roe v. Wade*]—and gave voice to the millions of women and men who want to make sure that abortion continues to be safe and legal (*NOW 1990*: 9).

Organizational opponents of the LDEF, such as Operation Rescue, a pro-life organization, which fell into NOW's disfavor, may also be singled out for attack by the organization. The 1990 Annual Report of LDEF claims: "We have fought to keep blockaders from keeping patients out of reproductive health care clinics, and we have won pivotal victories over Operation Rescue—including heavy fines for contempt of court" (*NOW 1990*: 9).

As a general-purpose women's-rights organization, NOW has a huge agenda. Some of the "action issues" listed in a 1991 document include: working to secure passage of the Equal Rights Amendment, promoting the rights of older women, working to end discrimination in education, working toward full economic rights for women, fighting for affordable child care for working parents, advancing the reproductive rights of women, protecting gay and lesbian rights, mobilizing against violence against women, protecting the rights of homemakers, seeking media reforms that would eliminate the portrayal of women as sex objects, advancing the cause of racial diversity, promoting military disarmament and a nuclear freeze, protecting the rights of physically challenged (disabled) women, and striving toward a clean environment (*Michigan NOW*: 1991).

As NOW's agenda demonstrates, women's groups, unlike other groups active in abortion litigation in the federal courts, tend to have a very broad focus (all issues relating to women). This broad focus makes them less effective in federal court litigation dealing specifically with abortion than other groups, such as Planned Parenthood and the ACLU's Reproductive Freedom Project. Women's groups simply do not participate enough in abortion litigation to be major players; their lack of participation renders them somewhat invisible. The indications are, however, that such efforts would be highly productive because in the handful of cases they were involved in, women's groups were highly successful. A more likely scenario is that women's organizations, as is currently the case, will continue to leave most of the abortion litigation to more focused major players, including the ACLU and Planned Parenthood.

Legal-Aid Groups

Table 4.5 (see page 77) lists all of the legal-aid organizations involved in abortion litigation in the federal courts during the 1973–1990 period, the cases in which they were involved, and their overall success rates.

An immediate observation is that only nine legal-aid groups became involved in the abortion cases, representing about 6 percent of the 165 total abortion-litigation groups. In addition, all of the legal-aid groups advocated a pro-choice position in the abortion cases. Legal-aid groups also enjoyed the highest success level of all groups in litigation, prevailing in 100 percent of the cases in which they were involved (see Appendix D).

Legal-aid groups are classified as public-interest groups because

Table 4.5

Legal-Aid Groups' Participation In Abortion Cases

Group	% Wins
Cases	
1. Black Hills Legal Services, Inc. *383 F.Supp. 1143* *402 F.Supp. 140*	100%
2. Community Legal Services *464 F.Supp. 483* *464 F.Supp. 487*	100%
3. East Denver Legal Services *389 F.Supp. 947*	100%
4. Legal Aid Society of Metropolitan Denver *389 F.Supp. 947*	100%
5. Legal Assistance Foundation of Chicago *469 F.Supp. 1212*	100%
6. Legal Assistance of North Dakota, Inc. *489 F.Supp. 238*	100%
7. New Hampshire Legal Assistance *406 F.Supp. 1072*	100%
8. New Orleans Legal Assistance Corporation *434 F.Supp. 1048*	100%
9. Office of Inmate Advocacy *643 F.Supp. 1217*	100%

these organizations exist for the sole purpose of providing pro bono legal services to indigent clients (that is, those whose incomes fall below federal poverty guidelines). The groups' funds tend to come overwhelmingly from the government, but not without some loss of control on the part of the legal-aid groups. For example, there are limitations on the types of cases they may become involved in and on their ability to engage in political activity, including advocacy.

In spite of these apparent constraints upon their political activity, one interesting finding is that the legal-aid groups examined in this analysis are "political activists" in the United States, when this is measured by involvement in such endeavors as lobbying Congress on judicial appointments, testifying before Congress on bills, financing Congressional campaigns, and meeting with agencies with regard to proposed rules and regulations. While the mean activism level for all groups was 44 percent, 50 percent of the legal-aid groups fall into the political-activist category. Further, out of eleven different types of groups, legal-aid organizations ranked third on the political-activism scale (see Appendix E).

Legal-aid organizations also tended to be small and resource-poor in relation to the other organizations that became involved in abortion litigation in the federal courts. While the average budget for all groups was about $11 million, legal-aid groups had small budgets of only about $2 million per year (n = 7). The groups also had few staff members, averaging only 77 when the overall mean for all organizations was 295 staff members. The utilization of volunteers by legal-aid groups was at about the same level as the aggregate usage. While 86 percent of all abortion organizations indicated they rely on volunteers, 87.5 percent of the legal-aid groups suggested they rely on the services of volunteers. Legal-aid groups also tended to be relatively young organizations. While the average age for all groups in 1992 was thirty-seven years, the average age for legal-aid groups was only twenty-six years.

Legal-aid groups, as might be expected, were repeat players in federal court litigation, ranking third out of eleven different organizational types on the repeat-player scale (see Appendix C). Also, while 23 percent of all abortion groups were frequently involved in federal court litigation, 25 percent of the legal-aid groups were frequently involved in litigation in the federal courts.

Not surprisingly, the legal-aid groups ranked at the bottom in terms of both the *amicus-curiae* (see Appendix G) and the policy-oriented litigation scales (see Appendix H). Specifically, abortion groups tended to use *amicus-curiae* filings as a sole means of participating in federal-court cases at a level of about 17.1 percent. In contrast, none of the legal-aid groups relied solely on an *amicus-curiae* litigation strategy (see Appendix G). The nature of legal-aid groups is that they are concerned foremost with their clients and become involved in federal court cases with the main goal of helping indigent clients. As such, I also expected legal-aid groups to have a low rank on the policy-oriented litigation scale, which measures the extent to which groups become involved in cases for the sole purpose of changing legal precedent. While 12.5 percent of the abortion organizations indicated that changing judicial policy was their main goal in litigation, none of the legal-aid groups listed this as their primary litigation goal (see Appendix H).

One advantage enjoyed by legal-aid groups in litigation is their high level of cooperation with other, similar groups. In fact, legal-aid groups ranked second out of 11 groups on an inter-group cooperation scale, which measures the extent to which groups interact with each other through informal exchanges of information, attending conferences, and joint litigation (see Appendix F). While the overall average on the measure of inter-group cooperation was 52 percent, 75 percent of the legal-aid groups engaged in high levels of inter-group cooperation.

Given that legal-aid groups enjoyed such a high success rate in the federal court abortion cases in which they were involved, a question arises: Why are they not significant players in abortion litigation? In fact, legal-aid groups became involved in only 7 percent ($n = 10$) of the 145 abortion cases examined in this analysis. The minor role played by legal-aid groups is explained by the fact that they are not specialists in abortion litigation, but only haphazardly become involved in federal court cases dealing with abortion when an indigent client comes to them with a concrete legal problem related to abortion. Once again, legal-aid groups are formed for the purpose of rendering free legal services to those otherwise unable to afford them, not for the purpose of promoting the abortion rights of women. Also, since federal restrictions on political advocacy by legal-aid groups exist and legal-aid groups rely heavily on government funding, it is not that surprising that legal-aid groups would decline to become visible pro-choice actors in abortion litigation in the federal courts.

Not-For-Profit Abortion Clinics

Table 4.6 (see page 80) lists the not-for-profit abortion clinics involved in abortion litigation in the federal courts during the 1973–1990 period, the cases they were involved in, and their overall success rates.

These twelve nonprofit abortion clinics represent only a small portion, close to 7 percent, of the organizations involved in abortion litigation. The nonprofit clinics, all of which advocated a pro-choice position in litigation before the federal courts, had higher than average levels of success. While the overall success rate was 81 percent, nonprofit clinics prevailed in about 85 percent of their cases.

Nonprofit abortion clinics are placed within the "public-interest-group" category because they provide a collective benefit—free or reduced-fee abortion and reproductive-health-care services—that is made available to non-group members.

Table 4.6

Not-For-Profit Abortion Clinics' Participation In Abortion Cases

Group	% Wins
Cases	
1. Atlanta Center for Reproductive Health, Inc. *471 F.Supp. 1326* *481 F.Supp. 46*	100%
2. Care Center of Springfield, Inc. *531 F.Supp. 320* *568 F.Supp. 1490*	100%
3. Crittenton Hastings House and Clinic *450 F.Supp. 997* *499 F.Supp. 215*	50%
4. Elizabeth Blackwell Health Center for Women *464 F.Supp. 483* *464 F.Supp. 487*	100%
5. Feminist Women's Health Center, Inc., Federation of *471 F.Supp. 1326* *481 F.Supp. 46*	100%
6. Midwest Health Center for Women *648 F.Supp. 756*	100%
7. Portland Feminist Women's Health Center *681 F.Supp. 688*	0%
8. Preterm *450 F.Supp. 997* *463 F.Supp. 222*	100%
9. Reproductive Health Services *481 F.Supp. 137* *483 F.Supp. 679* *655 F.Supp. 1300* *662 F.Supp. 407*	75%
10. Valley Family Planning *489 F.Supp. 238*	100%
11. Women's Health Center of Duluth, P.A. *648 F.Supp. 756*	100%
12. Women's Health Services *464 F.Supp. 483* *464 F.Supp. 487* *686 F.Supp. 1089*	100%

Although it was difficult to obtain financial information from the clinics, four of them responded to a question about their annual budgets. Of the four that answered, they reported that their mean annual budgets in 1992 was $1.2 million, which was considerably lower than the $11 million average budget for all organizational litigants. The main source of funds of these clinics is, in spite of their nonprofit status, patient fees, though these fees might be lower than those collected for similar services by for-profit clinics. More specifically, 66 percent (n = 8) of the nonprofit clinics suggested that their main source of funds is patient fees, another 17 percent derive most of their funds from the government, and 17 percent listed the main source of support as either private donors or foundations.

The twelve nonprofit abortion clinics tended to be small organizations, with an average staff size of only 39 members, as compared to the overall average of 295 staffpersons. The nonprofit clinics also fell behind others in their utilization of volunteers: 83 percent of these organizations used volunteers, as compared to an overall usage by groups of 86 percent. The nonprofit clinics tended, on average, to be younger than their organizational counterparts. While the average age for all abortion organizations in 1992 was thirty-seven years, it was only twenty-nine years for nonprofit abortion clinics.

It is not altogether surprising that the nonprofit abortion clinics ranked very low on the repeat-player measure of the extent to which groups are frequently involved in litigation in the federal courts (see Appendix C). These clinics are organized for the purpose of providing low-cost abortions and reproductive-health services. As such, the clinics have little incentive to become involved in litigation before the federal courts unless some vital interest is at stake, such as a state law that would restrict their funds or limit their operations. So the nonprofit abortion clinics tended to become involved in very few cases, and their appearances in federal court cases dealing with abortion may be best characterized as sporadic. While the overall organizational mean on the repeat-player measure was 23 percent, only 8 percent of the nonprofit abortion clinics suggested they are frequently involved in litigation before the federal courts (see Appendix C).

Whether due to a lack of resources or through design, nonprofit abortion clinics also ranked near the bottom on a political-activism scale (see Appendix E), which measures the extent to which groups lobby Congress on judicial appointments, lobby Congress on bills generally, donate funds to Congressional campaigns, and meet with agencies with regard to proposed rules and regulations. While the average score on this scale was 44 percent, only 25 percent of the nonprofit abortion clinics can be classified as political activists.

One of the only measures on which the nonprofit abortion clinics performed well, or above average, was the inter-group cooperation scale, which measures whether groups cooperate with other, similar groups via informal exchanges of information, attending conferences, and joint litigation (see Appendix F). While the mean on this scale for all organizational litigants was 52 percent, 58 percent of the nonprofit abortion clinics engaged in high levels of intergroup cooperation.

One of the nonprofit abortion clinics involved in the abortion cases examined here was Crittenton Hastings House, located in Boston, Massachusetts. Founded in 1836, the clinic has a staff of 125, relies on volunteers, and had a budget in 1992 in excess of $3 million. It is infrequently involved in federal court litigation. The organization provides many different services, all of which reflect a concern for women, children, and families. To this end, Crittenton Hastings House provides a full range of services: high-school education, job training, pregnancy prevention, emergency housing, child care, nutritional services, and medical care, including basic gynecological and prenatal health services. According to its 1990 annual report, "Crittenton's programs focus on preserving options and helping individuals to develop the tools necessary to pursue independent and productive lives" (*Crittenton 1990*: 1). Clearly, providing abortion and reproductive-health-care services to women is just one of the many tasks performed by Crittenton Hastings House.

One interesting point, however, is that the 1990 Annual Report makes no mention of the political agenda of the clinic. Also, a representative of Crittenton Hastings House suggested in a telephone interview in November 1991 that the clinic never engaged in lobbying Congress on judicial appointments, contributing money to campaigns, or testifying before Congress on bills. The representative also maintained that the only political activity the clinic engaged in was meeting with agencies about proposed rules and regulations, and even this was done infrequently. This nonprofit abortion clinic clearly identifies itself as simply a provider of social and medical services and leaves political lobbying efforts to other groups.

In contrast, a relative newcomer, the Elizabeth Blackwell Health Center, founded in 1975, is a nonprofit abortion clinic with a clear political agenda. As stated in its 1990 annual report:

Our staff and Board have taken an active role in advocacy work in the area of reproductive rights. Our Executive Director is the convenor of the statewide Pennsylvanians for a Right to a Private Life and is actively involved in the Southeastern Pennsylvania Abortion Rights Coalition (SPARC) which includes every major organization and agency in this region concerned with reproductive rights. A staff member serves on the board of the Greater Philadelphia Women's Medical Fund (*Elizabeth Blackwell 1990*: 5).

Still, the political-advocacy role taken on by the Elizabeth Blackwell Health Center is somewhat exceptional for nonprofit abortion clinics, most of which maintain low profiles, leading to an aggregate political-activism rank for nonprofit abortion clinics that is much lower than that of most other types of groups. Such a strategy may be necessary to ensure continued support of these clinics by public and private donors.

The main objective of the Elizabeth Blackwell Health Center, as with other nonprofit abortion clinics, is to provide high-quality gynecological services for women. In 1990 women made more than 7,700 visits to the Center. The main services provided by the Center include: direct medical services (including abortions), counseling, educational workshops, and public-education campaigns.

Nonprofit abortion clinics were not major players in abortion litigation in the federal courts. One major weakness is that they seem to be too few in number. Further, their strength is limited by highly visible and well-funded private abortion clinics and quasi-public/quasi-private clinics, such as Planned Parenthood, that have taken a leadership role in abortion litigation. The role of nonprofit abortion clinics in abortion litigation is also limited by their lack of incentive to engage in litigation in the federal courts unless a major organizational interest is threatened.

PRIVATE-INTEREST GROUPS

Planned Parenthood

Planned Parenthood Federation of America, Inc. (Planned Parenthood) and its affiliates have become, by the 1990s, some of the most visible and politically powerful actors in the pro-choice movement. Its political power can be traced to its economic resources, generated from patient fees, grants from private foundations, private donations, and support from the federal government. Planned Parenthood falls into the status of a quasi-public entity. Although Planned Parenthood is not officially a state agency, it is extensively regulated by the state and receives generous grants from the public sector. As a result, Planned Parenthood is best seen as a quasi-public/quasi-private provider of abortion and family-planning services.

The national office of Planned Parenthood is located in New York City. The organization was founded in 1916 and currently has 172 local affiliates. It is a huge organization, with 26,000 staff members, a budget of $331 million in 1992, and an enormous number of volunteers. Although initially resistant to both family planning and abortion, the current leadership of Planned Parenthood, including President Faye Wattleton, is strongly committed to family planning and abortion; in fact, Wattleton has taken the podium as a national spokesperson for the pro-choice movement.

One of the affiliates of Planned Parenthood, Planned Parenthood/World Population Los Angeles, Inc. (PPLA), sets forth in its 1990 annual report both its philosophical position on abortion and its "mission"; these statements parallel those of other Planned Parenthood affiliates and the national office. According to the report: PPLA "believes in the fundamental right of each individual, throughout the world, to manage his or her fertility, regardless of the individual's income, marital status, age, national origin or residence. We believe that reproductive self-determination must be voluntary and preserve the individual's right to privacy" (*PPLA 1990*: 1). So the mission of PPLA is:

> To provide comprehensive reproductive and complementary health care services in settings which preserve and protect the essential privacy and rights of each individual, regardless of the individual's ability to pay for such services. . . . To advocate, to an appropriate extent, public policies which guarantee these rights and ensure access to such services. . . . To provide educational programs which enhance understanding of individual and societal implications of human sexuality. . . . To promote research and the advancement of technology in reproductive health care and encourage the understanding of their inherent bioethical, behavioral and social implications (PPLA).

Hence, the local Planned Parenthood affiliate openly states that, aside from providing family-planning and abortion services, it also seeks to affect changes in public policy.

The 172 Planned Parenthood clinics located throughout the United States engage in the following types of activities: clinical services, community services, public affairs, and development. Their budgets tend to be in the $1 million to $3 million range. Clinical services are the main component of these Planned Parenthood affiliates, and they claim to provide high-quality, low-cost medical and surgical reproductive-health-care services, including abortions, tubal ligations, and vasectomies.

During the 1989–1990 period, for example, Planned Parenthood of Los Angeles (PPLA) rendered such services to 35,000 clients at nine clinics located throughout the Los Angeles area. PPLA plans to expand its operations, including opening twenty-one new clinics by the year 2000, to keep pace with the expanding population of the area (PPLA 1990). In addition, the clinics provided free AIDS testing and counseling, as well as general counseling and information on birth control, pregnancy, prenatal care, parenting concerns, and sterilization.

Most of the clients of Planned Parenthood clinics tend to be young and in the low-income bracket. In the case of PPLA, 62 percent of its clients, which include both women and men, were unable to fully pay for clinical services; their incomes fell below the official poverty line (PPLA 1990).

Relying primarily on volunteers and community groups, the local Planned Parenthood clinics also provided such community services as speaking to high-school students about family planning and birth control and providing information about Planned Parenthood and the services it offers.

Somewhat surprising is the extent to which local Planned Parenthood offices openly engage in lobbying or what they refer to as "public-affairs" activities, rather than relying for this purpose solely upon the political efforts of the national office. For example, PPLA suggests in its 1990 annual report: "In the aftermath of the 1989 *Webster* decision and the Governor's devastating two-thirds budget cut in family planning, PPLA's advocacy efforts were needed as never before" (*PPLA 1990*: 7).

The report continues:

> In cooperation with Planned Parenthood Affiliates of California and local
> family planning clinics, PPLA undertook a successful nine month cam-
> paign to restore funding for the Office of Family Planning. Strategies
> include grass roots organizing, state-wide Lobby Days, and a Pro-Choice
> Caravan to Sacramento on the anniversary of *Roe v. Wade*. . . . PPLA also
> played a key role in a successful lobbying effort to keep abortion services
> available to low-income women. For the first time in thirteen years, Medi-
> Cal funding for abortion was included in the state budget without restric-
> tive language (*PPLA 1990*: 7).

While the average budget for all of the organizations involved in
abortion litigation was about $11 million, none of the seventeen
Planned Parenthood organizations, with the exception of the national
office (which had an annual budget in 1992 of $331 million), reported
having a 1992 budget that exceeded this amount. Their budgets tended
to be relatively small, in the $1 million to $3 million range.

Similarly, Planned Parenthood affiliates tended to have relatively
small staffs. While the average staff numbered 295 members, Planned
Parenthood affiliates had considerably smaller staffs; none, with the
exception of the national office, reported a staff size of 295 or higher.
Most tended to have staffs numbering fewer than 100 members.

With regard to another presumed organizational advantage, longevity, the average age of all abortion organizations involved in the
survey was thirty-seven years in 1992. About 52 percent of the Planned
Parenthood affiliates were thirty-seven or more years old in 1992. Once
again, researchers suggest that organizations with longevity have an
advantage in litigation (Vose 1959; O'Connor 1980). And while only 86
percent of the organizations involved in abortion cases used volunteers,
all of the Planned Parenthood organizations indicated extensive use of
volunteers. Further, volunteers were utilized, as discussed earlier, in
significant organizational tasks, including fundraising for Planned Parenthood and engaging in educational efforts on behalf of Planned
Parenthood and its affiliates (PPLA 1990).

Because of these organizational resources, Planned Parenthood is
also one of the most effective lobbies in the pro-choice camp, with the
national office and even quite a few of the local offices becoming
involved in extra-judicial lobbying. For example, the offices testified

before Congress (or their state legislatures) on bills, met with agencies regarding regulations, and voiced their support or opposition to Congress on prospective nominees to the federal judiciary.

While 44 percent of all groups involved in abortion cases were highly involved in the political process (including testifying before Congress on judicial appointments, testifying before Congress on bills generally, financing Congressional campaigns, and meeting with agencies about proposed rules and regulations), 47 percent of the Planned Parenthood organizations appeared to be political activists (see Appendix E). While the national organization tends to focus its energy on lobbying the federal government, local Planned Parenthood affiliates are effective lobbyists at the state and local levels with regard to federal, state, and local policies that affect the reproductive and abortion rights of women. Further, as PPLA demonstrates, the affiliates' efforts to have an impact on public policies often meet with great success.

The Planned Parenthood organizations, through their advocacy, community service, and educational campaigns, acquired a high level of political visibility, which may serve to explain the preferential court decisions they received from the federal courts in post-*Roe v. Wade* abortion cases (Chapter 2). While the average success rate for all organizations was 81 percent, Planned Parenthood organizations prevailed in 82.4 percent of the cases they appeared in (see Appendix D). Table 4.7 (see pages 88–89) lists all of the Planned Parenthood organizations involved in the abortion cases analyzed here, as well as the success rates of the various Planned Parenthood groups in litigation.

The litigation strategy of Planned Parenthood organizations may be best described as offensive, in the sense that the organization and its many affiliates have an aggressive campaign that seeks to undo local and national measures obstructing the abortion rights of women (and, of course, the profits of the organization). Resources for litigation are available to this end, and Planned Parenthood became actively involved in the abortion cases examined here.

The seventeen Planned Parenthood organizations, which represent about 10 percent of all organizations that appear in this study, were involved in 35 of the 145 abortion cases, or almost 25 percent. The high visibility of this organization in the political arena is, therefore, mirrored in the judicial arena. Nevertheless, when organizational representatives were asked whether their organization is frequently involved in

Table 4.7

Planned Parenthood Groups' Participation In Abortion Cases

Group	% Wins
Cases	
1. Family Planning Clinic, Inc.	100%
594 F.Supp. 1410	
2. Los Angeles Area Council Planned Parenthood World Population	100%
368 F.Supp. 11	
3. Planned Parenthood Association--Chicago Area	100%
531 F.Supp. 320	
568 F.Supp. 1490	
4. Planned Parenthood Association of Cincinnati, Inc.	100%
635 F.Supp. 469	
5. Planned Parenthood Association of Kansas City, Missouri, Inc.	100%
483 F.Supp. 679	
655 F.Supp. 1300	
662 F.Supp. 407	
6. Planned Parenthood Asssociation of Southeastern Pennsylvania, Inc.	100%
401 F.Supp. 554	
464 F.Supp. 483	
464 F.Supp. 487	
508 F.Supp. 567	
686 F.Supp. 1089	
7. Planned Parenthood Association of the Atlanta Area, Inc.	100%
670 F.Supp. 971	
8. Planned Parenthood Federation of America, Inc.	86%
358 F.Supp. 1193	
421 F.Supp. 533	
491 F.Supp. 630	
633 F.Supp. 1123	
662 F.Supp. 407	
670 F.Supp. 971	
680 F.Supp. 1465	
9. Planned Parenthood League of Massachusetts	75%
393 F.Supp. 847	
450 F.Supp. 997	
463 F.Supp. 222	
499 F.Supp. 215	

Table 4.7 (Cont.)
Planned Parenthood Groups' Participation In Abortion Cases

10.	**Planned Parenthood of Central Missouri**	0%
	392 F.Supp. 1362	
11.	**Planned Parenthood of East Central Georgia**	100%
	670 F.Supp. 971	
12.	**Planned Parenthood of Minnesota**	100%
	648 F.Supp. 756	
13.	**Planned Parenthood of Rhode Island**	100%
	530 F.Supp. 1136	
	598 F.Supp. 625	
	598 F.Supp. 1374	
14.	**Planned Parenthood of the Rocky Mountains**	100%
	680 F.Supp. 1465	
15.	**Planned Parenthood of Utah**	100%
	680 F.Supp. 1465	
16.	**Planned Parenthood of Washoe County**	100%
	616 F.Supp. 322	
17.	**Planned Parenthood Organization of Metropolitan**	100%
	Washington, D.C.	
	726 F.Supp. 1483	

federal court litigation, or are repeat players, only 12 percent of the Planned Parenthood representatives responded affirmatively (and one of these was a representative of the national office), while the average organizational score on the frequent-litigator variable was 23 percent (see Appendix C). This suggests that the success of Planned Parenthood organizations in litigation is not linked as much to their repeat-player status as it is to their high visibility and to the fact that federal court judges, for the most part, are supportive of these groups and sympathetic to their message.

Earlier research findings (Chapter 2) supported these observations: the fact that a group is a Planned Parenthood organization is significantly related to litigation success when one controls for other factors, including whether groups are repeat players in litigation.

For-Profit Abortion Clinics Not Affiliated with Planned Parenthood

A total of 50 for-profit abortion clinics became involved in federal court abortion cases, representing 30 percent of the organizational litigants (n = 166) involved in abortion litigation. Since these private abortion clinics are for-profit entities, they are properly classified as private-interest groups. All of these groups argued a pro-choice position in the abortion cases. Table 4.8 (see pages 90–92) identifies these private

Table 4.8

For-Profit Abortion Clinics' Participation In Abortion Cases

Group	% Wins
Cases	
1. **Akron Center for Reproductive Health, Inc.**	100%
479 F.Supp. 1172	
604 F.Supp. 1268	
604 F.Supp. 1275	
633 F.Supp. 1123	
2. **Alexandria Women's Health Center**	100%
726 F.Supp. 1483	
3. **Atlanta Women's Medical Center**	100%
471 F.Supp. 1326	
481 F.Supp. 46	
4. **Birth Control Centers, Inc.**	100%
508 F.Supp. 1366	
5. **Boulder Valley Women's Health Center**	100%
680 F.Supp. 1465	
6. **Capitol Women's Center**	100%
726 F.Supp. 1483	
7. **Causeway Medical Suite**	100%
488 F.Supp. 181	
597 F.Supp. 636	
8. **Commonwealth Women's Clinic**	100%
726 F.Supp. 1483	
9. **Delaware Women's Health Organization, Inc.**	0%
441 F.Supp. 497	
10. **Delta Women's Clinic**	100%
434 F.Supp. 1048	
488 F.Supp. 181	
597 F.Supp. 636	
11. **East Gyn Center, Inc.**	100%
508 F.Supp. 1366	
12. **Fox Valley Reproductive Health Care Center, Inc.**	100%
446 F.Supp. 1072	
13. **Friendship Medical Center**	0%
367 F.Supp. 594	
14. **Gary-Northwest Indiana Women's Services, Inc.**	66%
418 F.Supp. 9	
421 F.Supp. 734	
496 F.Supp. 894	

Table 4.8 (Cont.)
For-Profit Abortion Clinics' Participation In Abortion Cases

15.	**Gyncare Associates**	100%
	726 F.Supp. 1483	
16.	**Hedd Surgi-Center, Inc.**	0%
	711 F.Supp. 439	
17.	**Hillcrest Women's Surgi-Center**	100%
	726 F.Supp. 1483	
18.	**Hope Clinic for Women, Ltd.**	100%
	579 F.Supp. 377	
	579 F.Supp. 464	
19.	**Jacksonville Clergy Consultation Service, Inc.**	100%
	696 F.Supp. 1445	
20.	**Mahoning Women's Center**	100%
	444 F.Supp. 12	
21.	**Meadowbrook Women's Clinic, P.A.**	100%
	557 F.Supp. 1172	
	648 F.Supp. 756	
22.	**Metairie Women's Medical Center**	100%
	597 F.Supp. 636	
23.	**Metro Medical Center, Inc.**	100%
	726 F.Supp. 1483	
24.	**Metropolitan Family Planning Institute**	100%
	726 F.Supp. 1483	
25.	**Mobile Women's Medical Clinic, Inc.**	100%
	426 F.Supp. 331	
26.	**Nassau County Medical Center**	100%
	409 F.Supp. 731	
27.	**National Family Planning and Reproductive Health Association**	100%
	679 F.Supp. 137	
28.	**National Health Care Services of Peoria, Inc.**	100%
	579 F.Supp. 377	
	579 F.Supp. 464	
29.	**National Women's Health Organization, Inc.**	0%
	475 F.Supp. 734	
30.	**Northeast Women's Center, Inc.**	100%
	665 F.Supp. 1147	
31.	**Northland Family Planning Clinic, Inc.**	100%
	508 F.Supp. 1366	
32.	**Northland Family Planning Clinic West, Inc.**	100%
	508 F.Supp. 1366	
33.	**NOVA Women's Medical Center**	100%
	726 F.Supp. 1483	
34.	**Orleans Women's Clinic**	100%
	434 F.Supp. 1048	
	488 F.Supp. 181	
	597 F.Supp. 636	

Table 4.8 (Cont.)
For-Profit Abortion Clinics' Participation In Abortion Cases

35.	**Pilgrim Medical Group** *613 F.Supp. 837*	100%
36.	**PLS Partners** *696 F.Supp. 788*	100%
37.	**Prince William Women's Clinic** *726 F.Supp. 1483*	100%
38.	**Reproductive Health and Counseling Center** *686 F.Supp. 1089*	100%
39.	**Surgical Arts Centre, Inc.** *519 F.Supp. 22*	100%
40.	**Westchester Women's Health Organization, Inc.** *475 F.Supp. 734*	0%
41.	**West Side Women's Services, Inc.** *573 F.Supp. 504*	100%
42.	**Women's Center for Reproductive Health** *696 F.Supp. 1445*	100%
43.	**Women's Community Health Center, Inc.** *477 F.Supp. 542*	100%
44.	**Women's Health Care Center of Cape Girardeau, Inc.** *670 F.Supp. 845* *681 F.Supp. 1385*	50%
45.	**Women's Health Care Center of St. Peters, Inc.** *670 F.Supp. 845* *681 F.Supp. 1385*	50%
46.	**Women's Health Care Center of West County, Inc.** *670 F.Supp. 845* *681 F.Supp. 1385*	50%
47.	**Women's Health Services, Inc.** *482 F.Supp. 725*	100%
48.	**Women's Medical Center of Providence, Inc.** *530 F.Supp. 1136* *696 F.Supp. 788*	100%
49.	**Women's Services, P.C.** *567 F.Supp. 522*	100%
50.	**Women's Suburban Clinic** *686 F.Supp. 1089*	100%

clinics, and lists the cases in which they were involved and the success rate of each clinic in litigation.

In the introductory pages of this chapter, I discuss an interview I had in November 1991 with Bill Baird, long a champion of reproductive-freedom rights and now associated with Parents Aid Society in Hempstead, New York. His most interesting comments relate to a growing tension between such abortion clinics as Planned Parenthood, which are recipients of generous government grants, and those abortion clinics that receive no such support. Baird claims that during the 1980s and the early 1990s Planned Parenthood clinics were intentionally located near pre-existing non-Planned Parenthood clinics. Baird asserts that, through this strategy, Planned Parenthood is attempting to drive its competition out of business and that it is, thanks to government subsidies, at a competitive advantage and can charge lower fees for its services. As a result, he suggests, private abortion clinics throughout the United States have been fighting losing battles with Planned Parenthood, which is rapidly monopolizing the reproductive health care industry.

In this analysis, I found that the pool of non-Planned Parenthood private abortion clinics appeared to be shrinking. By the time I attempted to contact representatives of the fifty abortion clinics involved in abortion litigation in the federal courts, 25, or 50 percent, could not be contacted or would not respond to a request for an interview. Nine, or 18 percent, of the clinics had been dissolved, including: Friendship Medical Center; Gary-Northwest Indiana Women's Services, Inc.; Hedd-Surgi Center, Inc.; National Women's Health Organization; PLS Partners; Women's Center for Reproductive Health; Women's Health Care Center of Cape Girardeau, Inc.; Women's Health Care Center of St. Peter's, Inc.; and the Women's Health Care Center of West County, Inc.

The overall success rate of these private abortion clinics in litigation in the federal courts was relatively high. While the mean success rate in the abortion cases for all organizations was 81 percent, private abortion clinics (n = 50) fared slightly better, prevailing in 86 percent of their cases (see Appendix D).

Unfortunately, of the twenty-five private abortion clinics that responded, only three provided information about their annual budgets in 1992, so it is not possible to make generalizations about the financial resources of these private groups. Other information was more easily forthcoming. The average staff size of the twenty-five private clinics in 1992 was 29 staff members, which was considerably lower than the 295 average staff size for all organizations appearing in the abortion cases. The private clinics also tended to be relatively new arrivals, which is not surprising given that abortion has only been legal in the United States since 1973. While the mean age of all organizational litigants in 1992 was thirty-seven years, the average age for private abortion clinics averaged only eighteen years. Unfortunately, private clinics had some difficulty in attracting volunteers: 86 percent of the total group of abortion litigants utilized volunteer services, while only 44 percent of the private abortion clinics benefited from volunteers.

The private clinics ranked quite low on the political-activism scale, which measures the extent to which groups lobby Congress on judicial appointments, testify before Congress on bills, donate funds to Congressional campaigns, and meet with agencies with regard to proposed rules and regulations (see Appendix E). Actually, private abortion clinics rank tenth out of eleven different types of groups on this measure. While the average political-activism score for all groups was 44 percent, only 16 percent of the private abortion clinics fell into the political-activist category.

The private abortion clinics also ranked low marks on the organizational cooperation scale, which examines whether groups engage in high levels of interaction with other, similar groups through informal exchanges of information, attending seminars, and joint litigation (see Appendix F). The mean score for all organizational litigants on this measure was 52 percent, while only 48 percent of the private abortion clinics engaged in high levels of inter-group cooperation.

Somewhat interesting is the very low rank of private abortion clinics on the repeat-player scale, which measures whether organizations frequently litigate in the federal courts (see Appendix C). Of eleven groups, private abortion clinics ranked at the bottom. While the average score for groups on the repeat-player measure is 23 percent, only 4 percent of the private abortion clinics are repeat players in litigation. This is due to the fact that owners of private abortion clinics prefer not to spend scarce resources on litigation and may be unable to afford the costs associated with litigation.

The typical abortion case in which private clinics were involved in is one in which, for example, a new restriction had surfaced in federal, state, or local policy that would seriously damage the clinics' interests. In such instances, the clinics had no alternative but to litigate because the threat usually carried the potential of impairing the profitability of the enterprise. For example, in *P.L.S. Partners, Women's Medical Center of Rhode Island v. Cranston*, 696 F. Supp. 788 (1988), the state legislature passed a law requiring abortion clinics to get special permits that were expensive and involved a time-consuming application process. In this case, two abortion clinics banded together to challenge the state law on the basis that it violated *Roe v. Wade* (1973) and was therefore unconstitutional. The district court agreed with the plaintiffs.

Similarly, a private abortion clinic, West Side Women's Services, Inc., was forced to file suit in another case, *West Side Women's Services v. City of Cleveland*, 573 F. Supp. 504 (1983), after the city of Cleveland passed a zoning ordinance that banned abortion clinics in retail areas. This would force the clinic to relocate to a new area and would probably also reduce the abortion clinic's profits because retail areas tend to attract high levels of traffic. The case was decided in favor of the clinic after the court found the local ordinance in violation of *Roe*.

When a private abortion clinic finds itself facing unwelcome local, state, or federal policies that place restrictions on it, the clinic has several options. One is to "go it alone" in federal court cases, which involves hiring a private attorney to investigate the matter and, if the case has merits, to develop a case. At any rate, the costs of litigation are borne by the organizational "one shotter."

Accordingly, you see in the progeny of *Roe* cases involved in this analysis, and particularly during the 1970s after the 1973 decision in *Roe*, that many private abortion clinics made solo appearances in the federal courts to challenge newly drafted restrictions on abortion rights. For example, in *Friendship Medical Center, Ltd. v. Chicago Board of Health*, 367 F. Supp. 594 (1973), the named abortion clinic made a solo appearance, contesting restrictive abortion regulations issued by the Chicago Board of Health. The regulations were upheld.

Another abortion clinic, Gary-Northwest Indiana Women's Services, Inc., was more successful in another case involving a solo appearance by a clinic: *Gary-Northwest Indiana Women's Services v. Bowen*, 418 F. Supp. 9 (1976). In this case, a state law requiring minors to get parental consent for an abortion was found to violate the privacy rights of women and was deemed unconstitutional.

Private abortion clinics also appeared alone in a number of other federal court abortion cases including *Gary-Northwest Indiana Women's Services v. Bowen*, 421 F. Supp. 734 (1976); *Delaware Women's Health Organization, Inc. v. Wier*, 441 F. Supp. 497 (1977); *Mahoning Women's Center v. Hunter*, 444 F. Supp. 12 (1977); and *Fox Valley Reproductive Health Care Center, Inc. v. ARFT*, 446 F. Supp. 1072 (1978).

In addition to making solo appearances to contest abortion restrictions, private abortion clinics increasingly began to make use of joint-litigation strategies starting in the late 1970s and continuing through the early 1990s. In these joint-litigation cases, two major patterns arose. First, is the "multiple-clinics" approach, where a number of local abortion clinics (usually in the same geographic area) band together to contest a restrictive abortion policy. This has the obvious advantage of spreading the costs of litigation among the various clinics, making it more affordable. Another advantage of this approach is that the clinics are usually few enough in number so that each retains a great amount of control over the conduct of the case.

A multiple-clinic approach was, for example, used in *Doe v. Busbee*, 481 F. Supp. 46 (1979), where three abortion clinics, the Atlanta Center for Reproductive Health, Atlanta Women's Medical Center, and the Feminist Women's Health Care Center, banded together in a successful challenge to a state law that banned Medicare reimbursements for all abortions except those necessary to protect the mother's life. And four other abortion clinics, Birth Control Centers, East Gyn Center, Northland Family Planning Clinic, and Northland Family Planning Clinic West, brought suit in the case of *Birth Control Centers, Inc. v. Reizen*, 508 F. Supp. 1366 (1981). Their efforts were rewarded with a decision that found a local law requiring abortion clinics to be affiliated with a hospital unconstitutional. Another similar case is *Margaret v. Treen*, 597 F. Supp. 636 (1984).

The second type of joint-litigation strategy employed by private abortion clinics from the late 1970s through the early 1990s may be referred to as the "multiple-organizations" approach since what usually happens in these cases is that many different types of pro-choice organizations become involved in the case. These cases tend to have lead or major players, including civil-liberties groups and Planned Parenthood, with the primary and sometimes only voice in the actual conduct of the case. Joining them in a subordinate position may be religious groups, women's-rights groups, professional associations and unions, public-interest groups, and private clinics, just to name a few. In these cases, the presence of these subordinate players shows federal court judges that the deck is stacked in favor of the pro-choice coalition. Of course, losses to the subordinate players, including private abortion clinics, result from this strategy, since they are left with little or no control over the case.

A good example of the multiple-organization joint-litigation strategy is the case of *Akron Center for Reproductive Health, Inc. v. City of Akron*, 479 F. Supp. 1172 (1979), in which a private abortion clinic, the Akron Center for Reproductive Health, was joined by three separate

ACLU organizations: the ACLU of Cleveland; the ACLU of Ohio Foundation; and the ACLU's Reproductive Freedom Project, which is based in New York City. With the ACLU's direction, Ohio's restrictive abortion law, which required parental notice and consent and allowed for warrantless searches of abortion clinics, was found unconstitutional.

By the 1980s, the multiple-organization joint-litigation strategy employed by pro-choice forces in abortion cases had gone into full swing, as major players in litigation routinely lined up subordinate ones for the purpose of loading the dice (or its equivalent), in abortion litigation in the federal courts. For example, in *National Organization of Women v. Operation Rescue*, 726 F. Supp. 1483 (1989), Planned Parenthood, NOW, and nine abortion clinics joined forces against a single pro-life defendant, Operation Rescue. The decision favored the pro-choice side. The role played by the abortion clinics was again subordinate to that played by Planned Parenthood and NOW.

When you evaluate the role played by private abortion clinics in abortion cases, it is clear that these clinics tend to be one-shotters in litigation and become involved in an abortion case only when a federal, state, or local policy that threatens organizational survival is passed. When compelled to litigate, these clinics make solo appearances or engage in joint litigation. Joint litigation takes place either through combining multiple clinics or multiple organizations. The latter strategy is becoming more popular in the United States and is likely to continue to increase in usage and popularity. In the multiple-organization approach, clinics defer to the major players in litigation, such as civil-liberties groups and Planned Parenthood.

Another compelling question relating to private abortion clinics, and one not answered here, is whether the trend of "disappearing" private abortion clinics will continue, leading Planned Parenthood to establish a monopoly in the reproductive-health services industry. Further, if this does occur, what are the implications for patients when it comes to the costs of reproductive-health services, their quality, and the range of choices?

Professional Associations and Unions

All of the professional groups and unions that appeared in federal court abortion cases during the 1973–1990 period advocated a pro-choice position. These groups are classified as private-interest groups because they seek to benefit only group members through their activities. For example, the National Medical Association, a national organization that protects the interests of medical professionals, engages in various types of lobbying activity, including interest-group litigation, for the sole purpose of benefiting the interests of group members. In an earlier analysis that controlled for a host of other factors (see Chapter 3), the fact that a group was a professional organization or a union increased the probability of its prevailing in abortion litigation by over 14 percent; however, this variable was not statistically significant.

Table 4.9 (see page 99) lists the professional associations and unions involved in abortion litigation in the federal district court cases examined here, the cases in which they were involved, and their overall success rates.

Three of the organizations listed in Table 4.9 are labor unions and six are professional associations. These organizations enjoyed higher than average rates of success in litigation. While the mean success rate for all groups was 81 percent, professional associations and unions prevailed in 83 percent of the cases in which they were involved (see Appendix D).

The nine professional associations and unions constitute about 5 percent of the 165 total organizational litigants involved in the abortion cases during the period in question. The professional associations and unions were involved in 10 out of the 145 total district court cases dealing with abortion, or roughly 6 percent of the total. They were not major players in abortion litigation before the federal courts.

For example, in the case of *McRae v. Califano*, 491 F. Supp. 630 (1980), the American Academy of Child and Adolescent Psychiatry was involved along with twenty-three other pro-choice groups, most of which were civil-liberties groups (including the ACLU), Planned Parenthood, women's-rights groups, and public-interest groups. A number of religious groups also fell into the pro-choice camp. This same pattern arose in the case of *McRae v. Mathews*, 421 F. Supp. 533 (1976), where twenty-two pro-choice groups appeared, including civil-liberties groups, Planned Parenthood, religious groups, and women's-rights groups. Three professional associations present played a secondary role and generally followed the direction set by the major players: the National Medical Association, the National Association of Social Workers, and the American Public Health Association.

Table 4.9

Professional Associations and Unions' Participation In Abortion Cases

Group	% Wins
Cases	
1. American Academy of Child and Adolescent Psychiatry *491 F.Supp. 630*	0%
2. American College of Obstetricians and Gynecologists, Pennsylvania Section *552 F.Supp. 791* *613 F.Supp. 656*	50%
3. American Public Health Association *421 F.Supp. 533* *488 F.Supp. 181* *679 F.Supp. 137*	100%
4. Associated Students for the University of California at Riverside *368 F.Supp. 11*	100%
5. Georgia Psychological Association *670 F.Supp. 971*	100%
6. National Medical Association *421 F.Supp. 533*	100%
7. Obstetrical Society of Philadelphia *401 F.Supp. 554*	100%
8. Rhode Island Chapter of the National Education Association *598 F.Supp. 1374*	100%
9. Rhode Island Federation of Teachers and Health Professionals *598 F.Supp. 1374*	100%

It is probable that, like religious groups (see page 62) professional groups and unions in such cases play a more symbolic role than anything else, merely demonstrating through their presence that the position of the medical community (or some other professional group) on an issue raised in a case involving abortion roughly parallels that taken by major players in abortion litigation, such as civil-liberties groups and Planned Parenthood. These major players perform the tasks of formulating overall legal strategies and presenting legal arguments to courts.

Occasionally, professional associations and unions play a more active role in an abortion case, usually when a major threat appears to the interests of group members. For example, the American College of Obstetricians and Gynecologists, Pennsylvania Section, filed suit in

American College of Obstetricians v. Thornburgh, 552 F. Supp. 791 (1982) after the state of Pennsylvania passed a restrictive abortion law that required parental and judicial consent for abortions. The lower court upheld the Pennsylvania abortion law. However, the organization fared better in a later case, *American College of Obstetricians and Gynecologists v. Thornburgh*, 613 F. Supp. 656 (1985), where a district court found a state law requiring public disclosure for abortion unconstitutional.

Once again, however, the general pattern was that professional associations and unions generally play only a symbolic role in these cases. This finding is supported somewhat by the fact that these groups tended not to be repeat players, or are only infrequently involved in litigation in the federal courts. In fact, on a repeat-player scale, professional associations and unions ranked near the bottom when the frequency of their litigation was compared to that of other organizations (see Appendix C). While the mean for all organizations on the repeat-player measure was 23 percent, it fell to 12.5 percent for professional groups and unions.

Professional groups and unions had relatively small budgets. While the average budget in 1992 for all abortion organizations was $11 million, professional organizations and unions averaged around $4.5 million (n = 8). Their staffs were also somewhat small; these groups had an average of 36 staff members as compared to 295 for the overall group. Professional groups and unions relied to a great extent on volunteers, with 87.5 percent of them incorporating volunteers into their operations, as opposed to 86 percent for all abortion organizations. One of the few advantages professional groups and unions shared is longevity. While the average age in 1992 of all groups was thirty-seven years, professional groups and unions averaged around seventy-six years.

Professional groups and unions also engage in above-average levels of political lobbying, which includes lobbying Congress on judicial appointments, testifying before Congress on bills, financing Congressional campaigns, and meeting with agencies with regard to proposed rules and regulations (see Appendix E). While the mean political-activism level for all groups was 44 percent, 50 percent of the professional associations and unions engage in high levels of political lobbying. These groups ranked third out of eleven groups on the political-activism scale (see Appendix E).

These groups fall slightly below mean inter-group cooperation levels for abortion litigants. While the average score on inter-group cooperation (which includes informal exchanges of information, attending conferences, and joint litigation) was 52 percent, 50 percent of the professional groups and unions suggested that they engage in high levels of inter-group cooperation (see Appendix F). Professional groups and unions ranked sixth out of eleven groups on an inter-group-cooperation scale.

One of the professional associations that made an appearance in the abortion cases examined here is the American Public Health Association (APHA). Founded in 1872, APHA had an operating budget in 1992 in excess of $5.5 million and sixty-five staff members. The main source of support for APHA is membership dues, although it also derives some support from the sale of publications and federal grants.

APHA is somewhat atypical in the sense that it, unlike most professional associations and unions, frequently engages in litigation in the federal courts. It is also somewhat active in political-lobbying activities, including: lobbying Congress on judicial appointments, testifying before Congress on bills, and meeting with agencies with regard to proposed rules and regulations. It is also highly involved in cooperation with other groups, through informal exchanges of information, attending seminars, and joint litigation.

According to a 1991 APHA publication:

The American Public Health Association (APHA) is a professional society, founded in 1872, representing all disciplines and specialties of public health. The Association's aggregate membership includes more than 30,000 members in 24 specialty sections that serve to develop the technical and scientific foundations of the Association's standards, policies, advocacy, professional meetings, and publications. . . . As the world's oldest and largest multidisciplinary organization of public health professionals and community health leaders, APHA has throughout its history been in the forefront of numerous efforts to prevent disease and promote health. These activities could not long survive without the voluntary efforts of its members. Their countless hours . . . have assured that the formulation of health policy and programs are based on scientific principles and sound health practices. (*APHA 1991a*: 1).

Of course, as an organization that generally promotes public health, APHA has many issues that compete for attention. For example, in an APHA list of "1992 Federal Legislative Priorities," the following issues, along with others, were included at the top of the list: abortion, AIDS, alcohol, tobacco, drugs, child-health issues, the environment, occupational health, family planning, the Fiscal Year 1993 Health Budget of the federal government and appropriations, injury prevention and control, national-health-program issues, health care for the uninsured, preventive health issues, and sexually transmitted diseases (*APHA 1991b*).

APHA's position on family planning and abortion is clearly stated: "APHA policy incorporates program guidelines and standards for assuring individuals' rights to information and counseling about reproductive options, access to contraceptives, and family planning services" (*APHA 1991a*: 6).

APHA successfully lobbied the federal government in favor of federal funding for Title X Family Planning Funds. The organization also lobbied the courts, including the United States Supreme Court, as this APHA publication suggests:

> The APHA has advocated for the right to information and access to family planning services through *amicus curiae* briefs in every Supreme Court case and numerous federal court cases, including: *Roe v. Wade*; *Webster v. Reproductive Health Services*; *Rust v. Louis Sullivan*; *NFPRHA, APHA v. Louis Sullivan*; *Ohio v. Akron Center for Reproductive Health*; and *Bowen v. Kendrick* (*APHA 1991a*: 6).

Another organization that participated in federal court cases involving abortion is the American Academy of Child and Adolescent Psychiatry ("the Academy"), a national professional association located in Washington, DC. The group was founded in 1953 to serve the interests of psychiatrists who treat children and adolescents. Since the Academy seeks to help group members only, it is properly classified as a private-interest group. In 1992 it had an operating budget of $2 million and a staff of seventeen, and relied on volunteers in its day-to-day operations. The main source of funds is membership dues.

This organization is more typical of professional groups and unions than the APHA Association in that it only infrequently engages in litigation in the federal courts. It is more involved in overtly political processes than judicial ones since the Academy frequently testifies before Congress on bills and sometimes meets with agencies about proposed rules and regulations. It also engages in high levels of intergroup cooperation, including informal exchanges of information, attending seminars, and joint litigation.

In 1992, the Academy issued a very strong policy statement in support of abortion, as follows: the Academy "recommends that there be adequately funded programs of education for pregnancy avoidance, elective abortion, and available contraception, and that psychiatric services be used where appropriate to aid in the interruption of this cycle."

As discussed above, the Academy was involved in only one abortion case, *McRae v. Califano*, 491 F. Supp. 630 (1980), where it played a completely subordinate role to major players, including civil-liberties groups and Planned Parenthood.

The final assessment of the role played by professional associations and unions in abortion cases, therefore, is that they are not major players in these cases because they have no incentive to be major players. Professional associations and unions become involved in an abortion case only when it directly affects a major interest of group members. For the most part, professional groups and unions play a symbolic role through their appearances in federal court abortion cases, in which they indicate to judges that, for the most part, they agree with the positions advocated in these cases by major players, including civil-liberties groups and Planned Parenthood.

Public Hospitals

One public hospital appeared in the abortion cases examined here, the New York City Health and Hospitals Corporation. It argued a pro-choice position in two of the federal district court cases and prevailed in 50 percent of its cases. Of the abortion organizations examined, the New York City Health and Hospitals Corporation is one of the largest and most prosperous. It was founded in 1970, has a budget in excess of $2 billion derived from the state and a staff of thirty, as well as an array of volunteers. It is not a political activist; that is, the public hospital does not lobby Congress on judicial appointments, does not testify before Congress on bills, contribute money to Congressional campaigns, nor meet with agencies with regard to proposed rules and regulations. It infrequently appears in litigation in the federal courts and engages in low levels of inter-group cooperation.

Although this public hospital is well-organized and has vast resources, public hospitals generally are unlikely to be major players in abortion litigation unless they derive a major part of their revenues from abortion-related services. But because few if any public hospitals fall into this category, it is probable that they will play only a minor and inconsequential role in abortion litigation in the federal courts. However, to the extent that they do appear, they will likely adopt the pro-choice position.

For example, the New York City Health and Hospitals Corporation appeared with twenty-one other pro-choice groups in the case of *McRae v. Mathews*, 421 F. Supp. 533 (1976), where the district court held, in accordance with their arguments, that a federal regulation banning Medicaid funds for elective abortions was unconstitutional. This case appears to be one in which major players in litigation that were present in this case, such as Planned Parenthood and civil-liberties groups (including the ACLU), load the dice by adding an array of pro-choice groups that do not contribute substantively to the case; however, the presence of these pro-choice groups shows that powerful interest groups are affected by the decision in question and that they are carefully scrutinizing the court's actions though their presence.

So the New York City Health and Hospitals Corporation was involved in this case for this symbolic, subordinate purpose as were a host of other minor players including, among others, various religious groups, professional associations and unions, and women's-rights groups. The strategy of the pro-choice coalition worked: the federal regulation was found to be unconstitutional.

But in *McRae v. Califano*, 491 F. Supp. 630 (1980), the same pro-choice groups with major and subordinate roles in litigation including the New York City Health and Hospitals Corporation, argued that the so-called "Hyde Amendment," which denied public funds for non-therapeutic abortions, violated *Roe v. Wade* (1973). The results in this case, however, were different. The law was upheld, and the pro-choice coalition was unsuccessful in its litigation efforts.

PRO-LIFE GROUPS

Despite the popular depiction of the pro-life forces as a strong and unified force in the United States, of the 166 total organizations involved in federal court abortion cases during the 1973–1990 period, only 10, or roughly 6 percent were pro-life organizations. The names of these organizations, the cases they became involved in, whether they are religious or public-interest organizations, and their success rates are all listed in Table 4.10 (see page 106).

The overall success rate for the ten pro-life groups was quite low, at 46 percent. Since the overall success rate for groups involved in abortion litigation in the federal courts during the period in question was 81 percent, the pro-life groups fared far worse than most organizational litigants in these cases. If you glance at Appendix D, which ranks the major types of organizations on their success in these abortion cases, you find that out of eleven different types of groups, pro-life groups rank number eleventh, or at the very bottom. In short, of all groups, pro-life groups had the worst success rate in abortion litigation in the federal courts.

It is also striking that only two, or 20 percent of these pro-life groups were religious organizations, since many people believe that the pro-life movement is dominated by religious organizations. Instead, 80 percent of the pro-life groups that appeared in federal court abortion cases were public-interest groups.

The pro-life forces are also, in relation to other abortion organizations, resource-poor, small, and weak organizations. While the average budget for all abortion litigants in 1992 was $11 million, the nine pro-life groups (one, Celebrate Life, was not available for an interview) confronted the overwhelming resources of the pro-choice forces with annual budgets of only about $442,000, most of which came in the form of individual donations. The pro-life groups also suffered from small staffs; while the average staff for all abortion groups consisted of 295 members, pro-life groups had an average staff of only 12. The pro-life organizations attempted to compensate for their deficits by utilizing volunteers services; 100 percent of the pro-life groups reported using volunteers in comparison to 86 percent for the larger group of abortion litigants. Pro-life organizations were also younger than most of the other groups that challenged them in the federal courts. The average age

Table 4.10

Pro-Life Groups' Participation In Abortion Cases

Group	% Wins
Type of Group *Cases*	
1. **Advocates for Life, Inc.** **Public Interest** *681 F.Supp. 688*	100%
2. **Americans United for Life Legal Defense Fund** **Public Interest** *448 F.Supp. 997* *469 F.Supp. 1212* *491 F.Supp. 630* *531 F.Supp. 320* *568 F.Supp. 1490* *579 F.Supp. 377* *579 F.Supp. 464*	14%
3. **Catholic League for Religious and Civil Rights** **Religious** *491 F.Supp. 630*	100%
4. **Celebrate Life** **Public Interest** *682 F.Supp. 162*	100%
5. **Christians in Action** **Religious** *681 F.Supp. 688*	100%
6. **(National) Constitutional Right to Life Committee** **Public Interest** *358 F.Supp. 1193*	0%
7. **Georgia Right to Life Committee** **Public Interest** *670 F.Supp. 971*	0%
8. **Minnesota Citizens for Life, Inc.** **Public Interest** *378 F.Supp. 1008*	0%
9. **Operation Rescue** **Public Interest** *721 F.Supp. 1168* *726 F.Supp. 1483*	50%
10. **The Rutherford Institute of the Georgia Legal Defense Foundation, Inc.** **Public Interest** *670 F.Supp. 971*	0%

for all organizational litigants was thirty-seven years, compared to an average age of only fourteen years for the pro-life organizations.

The pro-life groups were also at a disadvantage in relation to other abortion organizations because of their lack of political clout, low levels of cooperation with other groups, and their infrequent involvement in litigation in the federal courts.

Pro-life groups ranked ninth out of eleven groups on a political-activism scale, which measures whether organizations involved in abortion cases took part in extra-judicial lobbying including lobbying Congress on judicial appointments, testifying before Congress on bills, financing congressional campaigns, and meeting with agencies about proposed rules and regulations (see Appendix E). While the mean activism level for all groups was 44 percent, only 22 percent of the pro-life groups fell into the category of political activists.

Other abortion organizations clearly outperformed pro-life groups on another indicator, namely the extent to which groups engage in inter-group cooperation, including informal exchanges of information, attending seminars, and joint litigation (see Appendix F). While the average level of inter-group cooperation for all abortion litigants was 52 percent, only 11 percent of the pro-life groups engaged in high levels of inter-group cooperation, and the pro-life groups ranked tenth out of eleven groups on this scale.

Also, pro-life organizations clearly are not repeat players in litigation; that is, they are not frequently engaged in federal court litigation. While the average score for all abortion organizations on a repeat-player scale is 23 percent, 22 percent of the pro-life groups report being repeatedly involved in litigation in the federal courts (see Appendix C).

The typical litigation pattern for pro-life groups in abortion cases is that most of the pro-life groups are one shotters in litigation, meaning that they are rarely involved in court cases. Further, in a number of the federal court abortion cases examined, pro-life groups were brought in against their wishes and found themselves to be defendants. This occurred, for example, in *National Organization for Women v. Operation Rescue*, 726 F. Supp. 1483 (1989). In this case, NOW sought an injunction against Operation Rescue for the trespasses of its members at an abortion clinic; the injunction was granted.

However, not all of the pro-life groups became involved in the abortion cases as defendants. Some of the pro-life groups—particularly larger, national pro-life organizations—became involved in abortion cases by arguing in support of a restrictive state abortion policy. However, even in these cases, the groups suffered overwhelming losses. For example, the Constitutional Right to Life Committee had a success rate of 0 percent, and the Americans United for Life Legal Defense Fund, the most active litigator in the pro-life camp, had a success rate of only 14 percent.

It is telling to trace the litigation record in these cases of Americans United for Life (AUL), the legal arm of the pro-life organizations. In accordance with earlier comments, in most cases AUL argued in favor of restrictive state abortion policies but was quite unsuccessful in its endeavors. For example, in *Wynn v. Scott*, 448 F. Supp. 997 (1978), the ACLU faced off against AUL. In this case, the ACLU argued that a state (Illinois) law requiring parental consultation before a minor could obtain an abortion was unconstitutional. AUL defended the state policy, but the district court ruled in favor of the ACLU and against the parental-consultation provision.

Similarly, in *Zbaraz v. Quern*, 469 F. Supp. 1212 (1979), the district court considered the constitutionality of an Illinois law that prohibited the use of public funds for abortions except when medically necessary. Arguing in favor of the state policy was AUL. However, for the most part, the decision favored the medical doctors and three pro-choice interest groups that brought the action, the Legal Assistance Foundation of Chicago, the Roger Baldwin Foundation of the ACLU, and the Chicago Welfare Rights Organization.

AUL again acted as an advocate of state policy in *Planned Parenthood Association-Chicago v. Kempiners*, 531 F. Supp 320 (1981). Here, Planned Parenthood contested a state (Illinois) policy barring the transfer of public funds to any association, including Planned Parenthood, that offered abortion counseling and/or referrals. Planned Parenthood was joined by an abortion clinic, Care Center of Springfield, Inc. The court ruled in favor of Planned Parenthood and against the validity of the Illinois law.

The same pro-life and pro-choice groups faced off again in *Planned Parenthood Association-Chicago Area v. Kempiners*, 568 F. Supp. 1490 (1983), where the court, again favoring the pro-choice litigants, held that a state law (Illinois) denying state funds to centers engaging in abortion counseling was unconstitutional.

In *Charles v. Carey*, 579 F. Supp. 377 (1983), AUL again defended an Illinois policy requiring prospective abortion recipients to give "informed consent" to their abortions. The ACLU, aligned in this case with Hope Clinic for Women, an abortion clinic, argued that the law violated *Roe v. Wade* (1973). The district court agreed and ruled that the law was invalid. And in *Charles v. Carey*, 579 F. Supp. 464 (1983), the same groups argued over the validity of a restrictive state (Illinois) abortion policy, and the court held that most provisions of the Illinois law violated the constitution.

There was one notable exception to these decisions favoring the pro-choice stands. In the case of *McRae v. Califano*, 491 F. Supp. 630 (1980), decided by the lower federal courts, AUL argued in support of the so-called "Hyde Amendment," a federal policy that withheld federal money for nontherapeutic abortions, and the district court upheld the law. AUL actually prevailed. This win is even more notable because AUL had overwhelming organizational opposition. Among the groups appearing on the pro-choice side, were the ACLU, the Center for Constitutional Rights, Global Ministries of the United Methodist Church, NOW, and various religious groups. Perhaps helping AUL in this case was that the abortion policy was a federal rather than a state policy.

It seems to be quite rare for pro-life groups to join efforts in abortion litigation in the lower federal courts. Further, when they do, they are likely to face a coalition of pro-choice groups. So, in spite of pro-life groups' joint-litigation strategy, they may still be unsuccessful. This happened, for example, in *Planned Parenthood Association of the Atlanta Area v. Harris*, 670 F. Supp. 971 (1987). Two pro-life groups, the Georgia Right to Life Committee and the Rutherford Institute, appeared in the case and argued in support of a state (Georgia) policy that required parental notification before minors could obtain abortions. The district court found the law unconstitutional, which was the position also taken by a coalition of pro-choice groups, including: Planned Parenthood of America, Planned Parenthood of Atlanta, Planned Parenthood of East Central Georgia, the ACLU, NOW, the League of Women Voters, and the Georgia Psychological Association.

Pro-life groups tended not to have the luxury of resources and time to engage in policy-oriented litigation. Not surprisingly, pro-life groups ranked at the very bottom of all abortion organizations on a policy-oriented litigation scale (see Appendix H). Instead, in their litigation in the federal courts, pro-life groups had to respond to immediate threats to restrictive state abortion policies or to respond immediately to lawsuits in which they were named as defendants.

Overall, pro-life organizations are in a precarious situation with regard to their relationship to the "state." Although these groups have a common ideology in the sense that they are all committed to a pro-choice position on the abortion issue, in their abortion-litigation efforts these groups range from acting as agents of the state (when arguing to uphold current abortion policies) to flagrant violators of state law (for example, when pro-life group members trespass at private clinics).

One of the most important pro-life organizations in the legal arena is AUL, founded in 1972 and located in Chicago, Illinois. In 1992 the group had an operating budget of $250,000 and a staff of twenty, and relied upon volunteers.

AUL's only political activity consists of testifying before Congress on bills. It has relatively low levels of inter-group cooperation, and in a 1991 interview a representative of AUL suggested that the group was only infrequently involved in litigation in the federal courts. Despite this, in the sample of abortion cases examined here, AUL was the most active of all pro-life groups, participating in seven of the cases. Overall, however, it is quite ineffective in litigation; while the average success rate for all groups in the abortion cases was 81 percent, AUL won only 14 percent of its cases.

A 1991 AUL publication, however, gives you the impression that AUL was highly effective both in judicial and political arenas. AUL probably, of course, overstates its record in order to attract new members. The booklet states: "Today, Americans United for Life is known as the legal arm of the pro-life movement. As the oldest national pro-life organization in America, AUL continues to defend human life through vigorous judicial, legislative and educational efforts. The goal is to restore the right to life for persons at all stages, from conception to natural death" (*AUL 1991*: 1).

AUL's poor record in abortion litigation in federal district courts may be caused by AUL's stretching its limited resources too far, becoming involved in litigation before the United States Supreme Court and lower federal courts, drafting legislation for states and the federal government, and engaging in educational and public-affairs activities. Of course, AUL may attempt to "do everything" because it is one of the few viable pro-life groups in the United States with national stature.

As an example of its overextended agenda, the following is a partial account of the legal activities of AUL in the early 1990s:

> Since the first briefs that were filed in *Roe v. Wade*, AUL attorneys have made significant contributions to pro-life laws. AUL has participated in every Supreme Court abortion case since *Roe v. Wade*. . . . AUL's legal strategy to overturn *Roe v. Wade* and restore the right to life in America involves five main facets. AUL drafts model legislation for use at the state level which maximizes legal protection of unborn children and their mothers. . . . AUL writes and coordinates the filing of briefs before the U.S. Supreme Court and lower courts, and provides legal counsel to parties defending pro-life laws. . . . AUL represents key parties in the federal courts. . . . AUL provides legal counsel to state legislators and lobbyists and presents expert testimony during hearings in support of pro-life legislation. . . . AUL publishes law review articles and participates in a variety of educational activities (*AUL 1991*: 2–3).

Clearly, the agenda of AUL is too overextended, and few other pro-life organizations are in a position to effectively assist the organization. The cost of attempting to do too much is, as always, general ineffectiveness.

The Rutherford Institute is a pro-life group that might offer much needed assistance to AUL, particularly in the area of legal assistance. Many of the attorneys associated with the Rutherford Institute, including the founder and current chairman of the board John W. Whitehead, are preeminent constitutional lawyers with experience arguing before the federal courts and even the Supreme Court. As such, the Rutherford Institute could serve as an invaluable partner to AUL.

Of the pro-life groups, the Rutherford Institute is one of the strongest. Its operating budget in 1992 was $2 million, the highest of all of the pro-life groups. Its staff numbered twenty-seven, and it relied on many volunteers, particularly attorneys with expertise in arguing constitutional-law issues before the federal courts. Founded in 1982, the Rutherford Institute is also one of only two pro-life groups that are repeat players in litigation before the federal courts (the other is the Catholic League for Religious and Civil Rights).

Although the Rutherford Institute has the potential to be an effective partner for AUL, it is not because the institute has its own legal agenda, and abortion cases are only one of five types of cases that it gets involved in. In the federal court abortion cases examined here, the Rutherford Institute was only involved in one case, which it lost. The organization is also not concerned primarily with the pro-life issue but with the much larger issue of defending the constitutional rights of religious people (Rutherford: 1990). As explained in an informational pamphlet,

> The Rutherford Institute is a nationwide team of aggressive attorneys and concerned citizens dedicated to defending the constitutional rights of religious people. The Rutherford Institute operates a rapidly growing state-by-state network of chapters, providing legal services without charge to hundreds of people each year nationwide. Legal and educational services are targeted to five priority areas: 1. Preserve free speech in the public arena, including public schools. 2. Protect the right of churches, church schools, home schools and other religious organizations to operate freely without improper state intrusion. 3. Defend parental rights and family autonomy. 4. Support the sanctity of all human life. 5. Assist individuals oppressed for their beliefs in totalitarian countries (*Rutherford 1990*: 1)

The (National) Constitutional Right to Life Committee operates somewhat as a support group to AUL. The support this group offers to AUL is primarily educational, not legal, with the intent of influencing policy-makers and public opinion in the United States on the abortion issue and of gaining mass support for the pro-life position. As stated in a 1990 annual report of the National Right to Life Educational Trust Fund:

> One of the principal activities of the National Right to Life Committee since its inception in 1973 has been the promotion through education of respect for the sanctity of human life from fertilization to natural death. Consistent with that goal, National Right to Life's internal educational arm, the Trust Fund, offers a variety of programs . . . To improve personal and social awareness and responsibility for human life . . . To educate the American public about abortion. . . . (*National Right to Life 1990*: ix).

Of course, in addition to educational campaigns the National Right to Life Committee engages in other activities. One is becoming involved in litigation (although in the sample of abortion cases here, it appeared in only one). The National Right to Life Committee is, in relation to other abortion organizations, politically active because it contributes money to Congressional campaigns, testifies before Congress on bills, and meets with agencies about proposed rules and regulations.

The National Right to Life Committee, located in Washington, DC, was formed in 1973, had an annual budget in excess of $1 million and a staff of forty in 1992, and relied extensively on volunteer services. Once again, the effectiveness of the National Right to Life Committee as an ally of AUL is limited by the committee's myriad of political, educational, and legal activities. These fully occupy the resources of the organization and fill the time of its staff members.

Pro-life groups were fledgling, outcast groups in abortion litigation in the federal courts, with no friends, few resources, and low success in their litigation efforts. These groups suffer from little political clout, their tendency to make solo appearances in litigation, and their lack of support groups.

Compare the isolation of the pro-life forces with the many organizational friends of the major players in abortion litigation, namely pro-choice civil-liberties groups and Planned Parenthood. These friends include pro-choice abortion clinics (nonprofit and for-profit), pro-choice public-interest groups, pro-choice religious groups, pro-choice professional associations and unions, pro-choice women's groups, pro-choice legal-aid groups, and even a pro-choice public hospital. These friends provide material and symbolic support to the pro-choice civil-liberties groups and Planned Parenthood organizations. In contrast, the pro-life groups did not, for the most part, make effective use of the federal courts; this is demonstrated by the fact that pro-life groups had the lowest success rate of all groups in abortion litigation.

In addition to the other explanations offered for the poor record of pro-life groups in litigation, what might also hurt the pro-life groups is that they are in a precarious situation vis-à-vis the state. In these cases, they range from acting as agents of the state to overt violators of state law.

It is the pro-choice forces that utilize the federal courts, enjoy high success rates in their abortion litigation, and deal effective, repeated "blows" to the pro-life forces. In the abortion cases examined here, the federal courts were not friends of the pro-life litigants.

CHAPTER 5

CONCLUSION

BY THE EARLY 1990s, legal abortion in the United States is a fait accompli, although local adjustments will likely continue to be made for some time, corrected by the federal courts when local policies deviate too greatly from national standards.

Abortion, as a right of women—an extension of their right to privacy—was the concession of primarily white male policy-makers in the United States to the women's movement of the 1960s, just as a national policy of integrated public schools was an outgrowth of the civil-rights movement of the 1950s. After an uncertain beginning, abortion has now crystallized as abortion was commercialized during the last two decades. As abortion became a profitable business to medical professionals and those who offered abortion services and operated clinics, and because these interests were either already represented by organizations or formed new ones, the pluralist battle, as Schattshneider (1960) predicted, tended to favor the "haves" over the "have nots." The "haves" include those who are economically benefited by abortion and, as such, are very much pro-choice: Planned Parenthood, non-Planned Parenthood abortion clinics, professional associations and unions, and public hospitals. The "have nots," on the other hand, are the underfunded (or unfunded) pro-lifers, consisting of a motley crew of public-interest and religious groups who are seemingly motivated by their ideological commitment to protecting the unborn, although they fight an increasingly unwinnable battle.

Some extremists in the African-American community in the United

States suggest that abortion was adopted as a national policy as a form of genocide against African-Americans and other minorities in this country, and that the support for abortion stems in part from a cynical attempt to avoid providing social services and financial support to the progeny of these groups. The minorities' suspicions may be aroused as the federal government and state governments join in providing funds to such groups as Planned Parenthood, which operates abortion clinics across the United States. Support for these abortion clinics, including Planned Parenthood, also pours in from the private sector, most often as generous grants from foundations.

Of course, the pro-choice movement consists not only of a very well-financed and organized economic lobby, but also of numerous public-interest groups, such as broadly based civil-rights groups, not-for-profit abortion clinics, women's-rights organizations, and legal-aid organizations. One unexpected finding is that even religious organizations overwhelmingly supported the pro-choice position, with 89 percent of the religious groups involved in the post-*Roe v. Wade* (1973) abortion cases supporting the pro-choice position. Hence, the final step in the crystallization of abortion in the United States is the involvement of both public- and private-interest groups in supporting abortion clinics and the services they provide.

A popular myth, perpetrated by groups within the pro-choice camp and sometimes reported by the media, is that an organized and effective pro-life movement exist in the United States. In the early 1990s, the pro-life movement is weak, fractional, and for the most part, unfunded. The best indication of its weakness is that actors within the pro-life camp increasingly tend to resort to desperation tactics, such as blocking entrances to abortion clinics. Even these protest activities are anemic, occurring in such isolated regions as Missouri where public support for the pro-life position is higher than the national norm. Protests like these are easily squashed through arrests and judicial involvement. Groups, such as NOW, effectively identify seemingly dangerous pro-life groups, such as Celebrate Life, and then bring them to defeat and bankruptcy through the court system.

An overwhelming finding of this analysis is the lack of any meaningful organizational representation of the pro-life position in federal court litigation dealing with the abortion issue. There is quite an imbalance in federal court cases dealing with abortion from 1973 to 1990. The pro-choice side has an enormous advantage over the pro-life camp in terms of the number of groups that came to the federal courts to represent their interests. Specifically, pro-choice groups enjoyed a 6.5 to 1 advantage over pro-life groups in terms of the number of organizations that represented their interests in the federal court abortion cases examined here.

The pro-choice position also benefited from both the existence of numerous pro-choice coalitions and multiple representation by groups in federal court litigation; the pro-choice groups that appeared in the progeny of *Roe* cases include public-interest groups, civil-liberties groups, religious groups, women's-rights groups, legal-aid groups, non-profit abortion clinics, Planned Parenthood and its affiliates, for-profit abortion clinics, professional associations and unions, and a public hospital. The pro-choice groups also enjoy vastly greater financial, organizational, and legal resources than the pro-lifers, as well as greater visibility, because of their active involvement in political and judicial processes in the United States.

Pro-life groups share none of these advantages. Furthermore, in litigation efforts they find themselves in a precarious position vis-à-vis the state because pro-life groups appear in abortion cases both as agents of the state (when, for example, group members argue in support of a restrictive state abortion law) and as transgressors of the law (when, for example, group members trespass at private abortion clinics).

Abortion litigation in district courts is a lopsided affair, dominated by two types of pro-choice groups, civil-liberties groups (especially the ACLU) and Planned Parenthood, that have much higher success rates than most other organizational litigants. In the federal court abortion cases examined here, civil-rights groups prevailed in 87 percent of the cases they were involved in, and Planned Parenthood and its affiliate groups prevailed in 82.4 percent of their cases. The pro-life groups, on the other hand, had a success rate in these cases lower than that of any other type of organizational litigant, prevailing in only 46 percent of the cases they were involved in.

It has been argued that the success of the pro-choice civil-liberties groups and Planned Parenthood organizations in abortion litigation in the federal courts is probably linked to their high visibility. It is also possible that the pro-choice ideological message of civil-liberties groups and Planned Parenthood closely mirrors the position of members of the federal judiciary. Alternately, it may be that members of the federal judiciary are wary of the power of these groups and make their decisions in abortion cases with these groups' preferences in mind.

In contrast, pro-life groups are fledgling, outcast groups in abortion litigation in the federal courts, with no allies, few resources, and low success rates in their litigation efforts. These groups have little political clout, tend to be one-shotters in litigation, and lack support groups. In the abortion cases examined overall, the federal courts were not "friends" of pro-life litigants.

ORGANIZATIONAL SURVEY

1. IDENTIFICATION

   a. Name: _____
      _____

   b. Address: _____
      _____
      _____

   c. Phone Number: _____
   d. Is the organization affiliated with a larger organization? If so, please identify other organization:

      _____
      _____
      _____

   e. Year organized: _____
   f. Identify nature of organization: (Circle one)

      1. public-interest organization, defined as an organization that seeks to benefit non-group members
      2. medical-services clinic (includes abortion clinic)
      3. women's-rights organization
      4. civil-liberties organization
      5. professional associaton
      6. legal-services provider
      7. other (list): _____

2. NATURE OF BUSINESS

Describe main goal, operation, activity:

_____

_____

_____

_____

3. CONTACT PERSON/POSITION/DATE: _____

_____

_____

4. ANNUAL BUDGET OF ORGANIZATION: _____

5. SOURCE(S) OF FUNDS (PLEASE LIST): _____

_____

_____

6. STAFF SIZE

   a. How many paid staff members? _____
   b. Does the organization make use of volunteer services? _____

_____

7. LOBBYING ACTIVITY OF ORGANIZATION

Does the organization:

   a. become involved in litigation before the federal courts? (Circle one):

      1. frequently
      2. sometimes
      3. infrequently
      4. never

   b. Does the organization lobby Congress over the appointment of federal court judges? (Circle one):

1. frequently
2. sometimes
3. infrequently
4. never

c. Does the organization contribute money to Congressional campaigns? (Circle one):

   1. frequently
   2. sometimes
   3. infrequently
   4. never

d. Does the organization testify before Congress on proposed legislation? (Circle one):

   1. frequently
   2. sometimes
   3. infrequently
   4. never

e. Does the organization meet with agency personnel with regard to proposed regulations? (Circle one):

   1. frequently
   2. sometimes
   3. infrequently
   4. never

8. Has the lobbying activity of the organization increased/decreased in recent years? _____ If so, please indicate why:

_____

_____

_____

9. GOAL OF ORGANIZATION

When the organization becomes involved in abortion litigation in the federal courts, is its primary purpose to (Circle one):

a. help the litigants in question?
b. change legal precedent?
c. both?

10. LITIGATION STRATEGY OF ORGANIZATION

Which litigation strategy is employed by the organization (Circle one):

a. direct representation of clients?
b. appearance as *amicus curiae*?
c. a combination of the two?

11. COOPERATION WITH OTHER ORGANIZATIONS

Does the organization cooperate with other similar organizations through (Circle one):

a. informal exchanges of information?
b. exchanges of information through attendance at seminars?
c. joint litigation?

12. GENERAL COMMENTS (Please list any information that might add to an understanding of the organization, its function, activities, etc.):

_____
_____
_____
_____
_____

CODING FOR REGRESSION EQUATION

POLITIC: Measures whether organization is highly involved in political process

METHOD: To obtain this, I added mean scores of all groups (n = 126) on all four political variables:

Note: scores on these variables were:
(0) never (1) infrequently (2) sometimes (3) frequently

Extent to which groups lobbied Congress on judicial appointments: = .47

Extent to which groups contributed money to Congressional campaigns: = .22

Extent to which groups testified before Congress: = 1.07

Extent to which groups met with agencies regarding regulations: = 1.31

Sum of all four means = 3.07

Hence, on a measure of whether a group is highly involved in politics, those that had a combined total on these four political variables of greater than 3.07 were labeled as highly involved in politics and received a "1," while those below 3.07 were measured as not highly involved in politics and received a "0."

HICOOP: Measures whether group is highly involved in cooperative efforts with other, similar groups

METHOD: To obtain this, I added mean scores of all groups (n = 126) on the three cooperation variables:

Note: the scores on these variables were:
(0) no (1) yes

Extent to which groups exchange information with other groups: = .87

Extent to which groups attend seminars with other groups: = .71

Extent to which groups engage in joint litigation: .63

Sum of all three means: 2.21

Hence, groups that fell above the mean were labeled as highly involved in cooperative efforts with other groups and received a "1," while those falling below the sum of 2.21 on all three variables received a "0."

FREQLIT: Measures whether the organization is highly involved in litigation before the federal courts

METHOD: To obtain this, I simply examined the responses of groups to question and measured those that responded they are frequently involved in litigation with a "1," while those that responded they were involved only sometimes or infrequently, or never received a "0."

RANK OF ORGANIZATIONAL LITIGANTS ON REPEAT-PLAYER MEASURE

REPEAT-PLAYER VARIABLE: Measures whether the organization is highly involved in federal court litigation.

METHODS: I examined the responses of groups to the question of whether they are frequently involved in federal court cases; after this, I determined the mean response for all groups on this question; the mean is 23 percent.

REPEAT PLAYERS: Those groups above the organizational mean of 23 percent.

Type of Group	Rank	Frequent Litigators?
REPEAT PLAYERS		
Civil-Liberties Groups	1	73.7 percent
Religious Groups	2	29.4 percent
Legal-Aid Groups	3	25 percent

Type of Group	Rank	Frequent Litigators?
NOT REPEAT PLAYERS		
Pro-Life Groups	4	22 percent
Women's Groups	5	20 percent
Public-Interest Groups	6	14.3 percent
Professional Groups/Unions	7	12.5 percent
Planned Parenthood	8	12 percent
Nonprofit Abortion Clinics	9	8 percent
Abortion Clinics*	10	7.5 percent
Private Abortion Clinics	11	4 percent

* Abortion clinics include Planned Parenthood, non-Planned Parenthood for-profit, and non-Planned Parenthood not-for profit clinics.

Rank of Organizational Litigants on Success in Abortion Litigation in the Federal Courts

MEAN SUCCESS RATE: 81 percent

Type of Group	Rank	Litigation Success
Legal-Aid Groups	1	100 percent
Civil-Liberties Groups	2	87 percent
Women's Groups	3	86 percent
Private Abortion Clinics	4	86 percent
Abortion Clinics*	5	86 percent
Not-For-Profit Abortion Clinics	6	85 percent
Professional Groups/Unions	7	83 percent
Planned Parenthood and Affiliates	8	82.4 percent

Type of Group	Rank	Litigation Success	
Public-Interest Groups	9	67	percent
Religious Groups	10	52	percent
Pro-Life Groups	11	46	percent

* Abortion clinics include Planned Parenthood, non-Planned Parenthood for-profit, and non-Planned Parenthood not-for profit clinics.

RANK OF ORGANIZATIONAL LITIGANTS ON POLITICAL-ACTIVISM SCALE IN ABORTION LITIGATION IN THE FEDERAL COURTS

MEAN ACTIVISM LEVEL: 44 percent

Measures the extent to which groups are highly involved in the political process through: testifying before Congress on judicial appointments, testifying before Congress on bills generally, financing Congressional campaigns, and meeting with agencies about proposed rules and regulations.

Type of Group	Rank	Political Activism
Women's Groups	1	80 percent
Civil-Liberties Groups	2	73.7 percent
Professional Groups/Unions	3	50 percent
Legal-Aid Groups	3	50 percent
Religious Groups	4	47.1 percent
Planned Parenthood and Affiliates	5	47 percent
Public-Interest Groups	6	35.7 percent
Abortion Clinics*	7	28.3 percent
Non-Profit Abortion Clinics	8	25 percent
Pro-Life Groups	9	22 percent
Private Abortion Clinics	10	16 percent
Public Hospitals	11	0 percent

* Abortion clinics include Planned Parenthood, non-Planned Parenthood for-profit, and non-Planned Parenthood not-for profit clinics.

Rank of Organizational Litigants on High Inter-Group Cooperation Scale in Abortion Litigation in the Federal Courts

MEAN FOR HIGH COOPERATION: 52 percent

Measures the extent to which groups are highly involved in inter-group cooperation through: informal exchanges of information, attending seminars attended by organizational representatives, and engaging in joint litigation.

Type of Group	Rank	Inter-Group Cooperation
Civil-Liberties Groups	1	78.9 percent
Legal-Aid Groups	2	75 percent
Women's Groups	3	60 percent
Non-Profit Abortion Clinics	4	58 percent
Abortion Clinics*	5	52.8 percent
Professional Groups/Unions	6	50 percent
Private Abortion Clinics	7	48 percent
Religious Groups	8	41.2 percent
Public-Interest Groups	9	21.4 percent
Pro-Life Groups	10	11 percent
Public Hospitals	11	0 percent

* Abortion clinics include Planned Parenthood, non-Planned Parenthood for-profit, and non-Planned Parenthood not-for profit clinics.

Rank of Organizational Litigants on *Amicus-Curiae* Scale in Abortion Litigation in the Federal Courts

MEAN FOR *AMICUS* BRIEFS: 17.1 percent

Measures the extent to which groups in their litigation in the federal courts are solely concerned with changing legal precedent (as opposed to helping the litigant, or a combination of the two).

Type of Group	Rank	Policy-Oriented Only
Religious Groups	1	41.2 percent
Women's Groups	2	20 percent
Public-Interest Groups	3	14.3 percent
Professional Groups/Unions	4	12.5 percent
Civil-Liberties Groups	5	10.5 percent
Abortion Clinics*	6	1.9 percent
Legal-Aid Groups	7	0 percent
Public Hospitals	7	0 percent

* Abortion clinics include Planned Parenthood, non-Planned Parenthood for-profit, and non-Planned Parenthood not-for profit clinics.

RANK OF ORGANIZATIONAL LITIGANTS ON POLICY-ORIENTED LITIGATION SCALE IN ABORTION LITIGATION IN THE FEDERAL COURTS

MEAN FOR POLICY-ORIENTED LITIGATION: 12.5 percent

Measures the extent to which groups in their litigation in the federal courts are solely concerned with changing legal precedent (as opposed to helping the litigant, or a combination of the two).

Type of Group	Rank	Policy-Oriented Only
Religious Groups	1	41.2 percent
Women's Groups	2	20 percent
Public-Interest Groups	3	14.3 percent
Professional Groups/Unions	4	12.5 percent
Civil-Liberties Groups	5	10.5 percent
Abortion Clinics*	6	1.9 percent
Legal-Aid Groups	7	0 percent
Public Hospitals	7	0 percent
Pro-Life Groups	7	0 percent

* Abortion clinics include Planned Parenthood, non-Planned Parenthood for-profit, and non-Planned Parenthood not-for profit clinics.

BIBLIOGRAPHY

ACLU 1990. *Annual Report 1990 Reproductive Freedom Project*. New York: American Civil Liberties Union Foundation, 1990.

ACLUNC 1990. *ACLU Highlights of the Legal Program*. San Francisco: American Civil Liberties Union of Northern California, 1990.

Aldrich, J. and Cnudde, C. "Probing the Bounds of Conventional Wisdom: A Comparison of Regression, Probit, and Discriminant Analysis." *American Journal of Political Science* 19 (1975): 571–608.

Allen, F. A. "Legal Values and the Rehabilitative Ideal." In *Sentencing*, edited by H. Gross and A. Von Hirsch, pp. 110–117. New York: Oxford University Press, 1981.

American Academy 1992. *Policy Statement*. Published by the American Academy of Child and Adolescent Psychiatry. Position paper on Adolescent Pregnancy and Abortion, Washington, DC, 1992.

Americans United 1991. Organizational pamphlet. Silver Spring, MD: Americans United for Separation of Church and State, 1991.

APHA 1991a. *Leaders in Prevention*. Published by the American Public Health Association. Washington, DC, 1991.

APHA 1991b. "1992 Federal Legislative Priorities." Published by the American Public Health Association, Washington, DC, 1991.

Appleton, Susan F. "Beyond the Limits of Reproductive Choice." *Columbia Law Review* 81 (4): 721–758.

Atkins, B. M. "Decision-Making Rules and Judicial Strategy on the United States Courts of Appeals." *Western Political Quarterly* 25 (1972): 626–642.

AUL 1991. *Restoring the Right to Life Through Law and Education*. Published by Americans United for Life Legal Defense Fund, Chicago, IL, 1991.

Austin, T. L. "The Influence of Legal and Extra-Legal Factors on Sentencing Dispositions in Rural, Semi-Rural and Urban Counties." Ann Arbor, MI: University Microfilms International, 1980.

Bardach, E. *The Implementation Game*. Cambridge, MA: The MIT Press, 1984.

Bassiouni, M. Cherif. *International Extradition*. New York: Oceana Publications, Inc., 1983.

Basta. National newsletter of the Chicago Religious Task Force on Central America, June 1986.

_____. National newsletter of the Chicago Religious Task Force on Central America, June 1987.

_____. National newsletter of the Chicago Religious Task Force on Central America, September 1986.

_____. National newsletter of the Chicago Religious Task Force on Central America, December 1985.

_____. National newsletter of the Chicago Religious Task Force on Central America, December 1986.

_____. National newsletter of the Chicago Religious Task Force on Central America, December 1987.

Baum, Lawrence. *The Supreme Court*. Washington, DC: Congressional Quarterly, Inc., 1989.

_____. *American Courts: Process & Policy*. Boston: Houghton-Mifflin Company, 1990.

Beiser, Edward N. "The Rhode Island Supreme Court: A Well-Integrated Political System." In *American Court Systems*, edited by S. Goldman and A. Sarat, pp. 470–479. San Francisco: W. H. Freeman and Company.

Berman, David R. *American Government, Politics and Policy Making*. Englewood Cliffs, NJ: Prentice Hall, 1988.

Berry, Jeffrey M. *The Interest Group Society*. Scott, Foresman and Company, 1989.

Blank, Robert H. "Judicial Decision Making and Biological Fact: Roe v. Wade and the Unresolved Question of Fetal Viability." *Western Political Quarterly* 37 (1984): 584–602.

Blum, C. "The Ninth Circuit and the Protection of Asylum Since the Passage of the Refugee Act of 1980." *San Diego Law Review* 23 (1986): 327–373.

Bolce, Louis. "Abortion and Presidential Elections: The Impact of Public Perceptions of Party and Candidate Positions." *Presidential Studies Quarterly* 18 (1988): 815–829.

Bowker, L. H. *Women, Crime, and the Criminal Justice System*. Lexington, MA: Lexington Books, 1978.

Briggs, Vernon. *Immigration Policy and the American Labor Force*. Baltimore: Johns Hopkins University Press, 1984.

Bryne, Stephen. *Irish Emigration to the United States*. New York: Arno Press and the *New York Times*, 1969.

Bryner, Gary C. *Bureacratic Discretion*. Elmsford, NY: Pergamon Press, 1987.

Burek, Deborah M., Koek, Karen E., and Novallo, Annette, eds. *Encyclopedia of Associations 1990*. Vol. 1, Part 3. Detroit: Gale Research Inc., 1989.

Burton, William L. *Melting Pot Soldiers*. Ames, IA: Iowa State University Press, 1988.

Caldeira, Gregory C. "Judicial Incentives." In *Courts, Law, and Judicial Processes*, edited by S. S. Ulmer, pp. 143–149. New York: Free Press, 1981.

———. "Public Opinion and the U. S. Supreme Court: FDR's Court-packing Plan." *American Political Science Review* 81 (1987): 1139–1154.

Carp, R., and Rowland, C. *Policy Making and Politics in the Federal District Courts*. Knoxville, TN: University of Tennessee Press, 1983.

Carrington, D. "U. S. Appeals in Civil Cases: A Field and Statistical Study." *Houston Law Review* 11 (1974): 1101–1129.

Carroll, J., Perkowitz, W., Lurigio, A., and Weaver, F. "Sentencing Goals, Causal Attributions, Ideology, and Personality." *Journal of Personality and Social Psychology* 52 (1987): pp. 107–118.

Carter, Lief H. *Administrative Law and Politics*. Boston: Little, Brown & Company, 1983.

Casper, Jonathan D. "The Public Defender: Man in the Middle." In *Courts, Law, and Judicial Processes*, edited by S. S. Ulmer, pp. 87–94. New York: Free Press, 1981.

Catholic Agitator, August 1984.

Catholics for a Free Choice. *Conscience*, a Newsjournal of Prochoice Catholic Opinion. Washington, DC: Catholics for a Free Choice, Vol. XII, September/October 1991.

Center for American Woman and Politics (CAWP), National Information Bank on Women in Public Office (NIB), Eagleton Institute of Politics, Rutgers University.

Central America Resource Center. *Directory of Central America Organizations*. Austin, TX, 1984.

———. *Directory of Central America Organizations*. Austin, TX, 1985.

———. *Directory of Central America Organizations*. Austin, TX, 1987.

Chiswick, Barry R. "Guidelines for the Reform of Immigration Policy." In *Essays in Contemporary Economic Problems: Demand, Productivity, and Population*, edited by the American Enterprise Institute for Public Policy Research, pp. 309–347. Washington, DC, 1981.

———. "Is the New Immigration Less Skilled Than the Old?" *Journal Of Labor Economics* 4 (1986): 165–192.

Choice. *1990 Annual Report*. Philadelphia: Concern for Health Options: Information, Care and Education, Inc., 1990.

————. Organizational pamphlet. Philadelphia, Pennsylvania: Concern for Health Options: Information, Care and Education, Inc., 1991.

Chomsky, Noam. 1983. *The Fateful Triangle*. Boston: South End Press, 1983.

Clarke, Alan. "Moral Protest, Status Defense and the Anti-Abortion Campaign." *British Journal Of Sociology* 38 (1987): 235–253.

Cockburn, Alexander. "Aborted Justice." *New Statesman & Society* 2 (July 14, 1989): 19–20.

Combs, Michael W., and Welch, Susan. "Blacks, Whites, and Attitudes Toward Abortion." *Public Opinion Quarterly* 46 (1982): 510–520.

Congressional Quarterly 1988. *Congress A to Z*. Washington, DC: Congressional Quarterly, 1988.

Congressional Quarterly 1973–1990. *Congressional Quarterly Almanac*. Washington, DC: Congressional Quarterly, Vol. 29–45, 1973–1990.

Cook, Beverly B. "Public Opinion and Federal Judicial Policy." *Journal of Political Science* 2 (1977): 567–600.

————. "Sentencing Behavior of Federal Judges—Draft Cases—1972." *Courts, Law, and Judicial Processes*, edited by S. Ulmer, pp. 462–469. New York: Free Press, 1981.

Cook, B. B., Goldstein, L. F., O'Connor, K., and Talarico, Susette M. *Women in the Judicial Process*. Washington, DC: The American Political Science Association, 1988.

Cooper, C., Kelley, D., and Larson, S. "Judicial and Executive Discretion in the Sentencing Process: Analysis of State Felony Code Provisions." Washington, DC: American University, Washington College of Law, 1982.

Council of State Governments 1988. *State Elective Officials and the Legislatures 1987–1988*. Lexington: Council of State Government, 1987.

Crites, L. L., and Hepperle, W. L. eds. *Women, the Courts, and Equality*. Beverly Hills: Sage Publications, 1987.

Crittenton 1990. *Annual Report 1990*. Boston: The Crittenton Hastings House, 1990.

CRTFCA 1988. *Information pamphlet*. Chicago: Chicago Religious Task Force on Central America, 1988.

Cummings, Milton C., Jr., and Wise, David. *Democracy Under Pressure*. San Diego: Harcourt, Brace, Jovanovich, 1985.

Dahl, R. A. *Preface to Democratic Theory*. Chicago: University of Chicago Press, 1956.

————. *Who Governs?* New Haven: Yale University Press, 1961.

Daly, K. "Discrimination in the Criminal Courts: Family, Gender, and the Problem of Equal Treatment." *Social Forces* 66 (1987): 152–175.

Damas, R. Y. "To Return the Persecuted to the Source, the Origin, the Cause of Their Suffering Is an Act of Injustice in the Eyes of Christian Love." *Basta* (December 1986): 24–25.

Danelski, David J. "The Influence of the Chief Justice in the Decisional Process of the Supreme Court." In *American Court Systems*, edited by S. Goldman and A. Sarat, pp. 506–519. San Francisco: W. H. Freeman and Company, 1978.

————. "Values as Variables in Judicial Decision Making." In *Courts, Law, and Judicial Processes*, edited by S. S. Ulmer, pp. 397–402. New York: Free Press, 1981.

Davidson, Roger H., and Oleszek, Walter J. *Congress and Its Members*. Washington, DC: Congressional Quarterly Press, 1981.

Dawson, R. O. *Sentencing: The Decision as to Type, Length and Conditions of Sentence*. Boston: Little, Brown and Company, 1969.

Department of Corrections 1988. "Report of the Overcrowding Task Force." Department of Corrections, State of Vermont, November 17, 1988.

Doe v. Bolton, 410 U.S. 179 (1973).

Dolbeare, Kenneth M. "The Federal District Courts and Urban Public Policy." In *American Court Systems*, edited by S. Goldman and A. Sarat, pp. 535–545. San Francisco: W. H. Freeman and Company, 1978.

Dornette, W. Stuart, and Cross, Robert R. *Federal Judiciary Almanac 1986*. New York: John Wiley & Sons, 1986.

Downs, Anthony. *An Economic Theory of Democracy*. New York: Harper, 1957.

Dudley, Robert L. "State High Court Decision Making in Pornography Cases." Prepared for delivery at the 1989 Annual Meeting of the American Political Science Association, Atlanta, GA.

Dye, T. R. *Politics, Economics, and the Public: Policy Outcomes in the American States*. Chicago: Rand McNally and Co., 1966.

Eagleton, Clyde. 1957. *International Government*. New York: Ronald Press Company.

Easton, David. *The Political System*. New York: Knopf, 1965.

Edwards, C. *Hugo Grotius, The Miracle of Holland*. Chicago: Nelson Hall, 1981.

Edwards, C. L. "Political Asylum and Withholding of Deportation: Defining the Appropriate Standard of Proof Under the Refugee Act of 1980." *San Diego Law Review* 21 (1983): 171–184.

Eisenstadt v. Baird, 405 U.S. 434 (1972).

Elazar, D. *American Federalism: A View from the States*. New York: Thomas Y. Crowell Company, 1972.

Elizabeth Blackwell 1990. *1990 Annual Report*. Philadelphia: Elizabeth Blackwell Health Center for Women, 1990.

Engel, M. *State and Local Politics*. New York: St. Martins Press, 1985.

Epstein, Lee. *Conservatives in Court*. Knoxville, TN: University of Tennessee Press, 1985.

Extradition Act of U.S., 18 U.S.C. 3184–3194; as amended November 18, 1988, P.L. 100–690, Title VII, Subtitle B, Section 7087, 102 Stat. 4409.

Farrell, Michael. *Sheltering the Fugitive?* Dublin, Ireland: The Mercier Press, 1985.

Forst, Martin L. *Sentencing Reform*. Beverly Hills: Sage Publications, 1982.

Frank, Jerome. "Facts Are Guesses." In *American Court Systems*, edited by S. Goldman and A. Sarat, pp. 310–316. San Francisco: W. H. Freeman and Company, 1978.

Frankel, Marvin E. *Criminal Sentences*. New York: Hill and Wang, 1973.

Franklin, Charles H., and Kosaki, Liane C. "Republican Schoolmaster: The U.S. Supreme Court, Public Opinion, and Abortion." *American Political Science Review* 83 (1989): 751–771.

Freeman, Joe. *The Politics of Women's Liberation*. Chicago: University of Chicago Press, 1975.

Galanter, M. "Why the 'Haves' Come Out Ahead: Speculation on the Limits of Social Change." *Law and Society Review* 9 (1974): 85–160.

———. "Who Wins?" In *American Court Systems*, edited by S. Goldman and A. Sarat. San Francisco: W. H. Freeman and Company, 1978.

Garraty, John A. *Quarrels That Have Shaped the Constitution*. New York: Harper & Row, 1987.

Gibson, James L. "Discriminant Functions, Role Orientations and Judicial Behavior: Theoretical and Methodological Linkages." *Journal of Politics* 37 (1977): 917–936.

Giles, M. W. and Walker, T. G. "Judicial Policy-Making and Southern School Segregation." In *American Court Systems*, edited by S. Goldman and A. Sarat, pp. 386–395. San Francisco: W. H. Freeman and Company, 1978.

Glick, Henry R. *Courts, Politics and Justice*. New York: McGraw-Hill, 1988.

———. *Courts In American Politics*. New York: McGraw-Hill, 1990.

Golden, R., and McConnell, M. *Sanctuary: The New Underground Railroad*. New York: Orbis Books, 1986.

Goldman, Sheldon. "Voting Behavior on the U.S. Court of Appeals." *American Political Science Review* 69 (1975): 491–506.

———. "Voting Behavior on the United States Courts of Appeals Revisited." In *American Court Systems*, edited by S. Goldman and A. Sarat, pp. 396–411. San Francisco: W. H. Freeman and Company, 1978.

Goldstein, J. "The Political Economy of Trade: Institutions of Protection." *American Political Science Review* 80 (1986): 161–184.

Gottfredson, D. M. "Sentencing Guidelines." In *Sentencing*, edited by H.

Gross and A. Von Hirsch, pp. 310–314. New York: Oxford University Press, 1981.

Gottfredson, D. M. and Gottfredson, M. R. *Decisionmaking in Criminal Justice*. Cambridge: Ballinger, 1980.

Gottfredson, D. M., Wilkins, L., and Hoffman, P. "Policy Implications of Guidelines." In *Sentencing*, edited by H. Gross and A. Von Hirsch, pp. 315–317. New York: Oxford University Press, 1981.

Graber, Mark A. "Interpreting Abortion." Prepared for delivery at the 1990 Annual Meeting of the American Political Science Association, San Francisco, California, August 30–September 2, 1990.

Graeber, Dorothy. "Judicial Activity and Public Attitude." *Buffalo Law Review* 23 (1973): 465–497.

Granberg, Donald. "An Anomaly in Political Perception." *Public Opinion Quarterly* 49 (1985): 504–516.

Griswold, D. "Deviation from Sentencing Guidelines: The Issue of Unwarranted Disparity." *Journal of Criminal Justice* 15 (1987): 317–329.

Griswold v. Connecticut, 381 U.S. 479 (1965).

Gross, H., and Von Hirsch, A. *Sentencing*. New York: Oxford University Press, 1981.

Gryski, Gerald S., Main, Eleanor C., and Dixon, William J. "Models of State Court High Decision Making in Sex Discrimination Cases." *Journal of Politics* 48 (1986): 143–155.

Hagan, J. "Law, Order and Sentencing: A Study of Attitude in Action." *Sociometry* 38 (1975): 347.

————. "Review Essay: A Great Truth in the Study of Crime." *Criminology* 25 (1987): 421–428.

Haire, Susan, and Songer, Donald R. "A Multivariate Model of Voting on the United States Courts of Appeals." Prepared for delivery at the 1990 annual meeting of the Midwest Political Science Association, the Palmer House Hotel, Chicago, IL, April 7, 1990.

Hall, Jeffrey A. "A Recommended Approach to Bail in International Extradition Cases." *Michigan Law Review* 86 (1987): 599.

Harris, David. "The Right to a Fair Trial in Criminal Proceedings as a Human Right." *International and Comparative Law Quarterly* 16 (1967): 352–378.

Heclo, H. "Issue Networks and the Executive Establishment." In *The New American Political System*, edited by A. King, pp. 161–185. Washington, DC: American Enterprise Institute, 1978.

Helton, A. C. "Political Asylum Under the 1980 Refugee Act: An Unfulfilled Promise." *University of Michigan Law Reference* 17 (1984): 243–264.

————. "The Proper Role of Discretion in Political Asylum Determinations." *San Diego Law Review* 22 (1985): 999–1020.

Higgins, Rosalyn. *The Development of International Law Through the Political Organs of the United Nations*. New York: Oxford University Press, 1963.

Hildreth, Anne, and Dran, Ellen M. "How Women Define Women's Interests: Abortion and Gender Mobilization in Illinois." Paper presented at the annual meeting of the Midwest Political Science Association, Chicago, IL April 6, 1990.

Hofferbert, Richard I. *The Study of Public Policy*. New York: Bobbs-Merrill Company, Inc., 1974.

Horan, Dennis J. "Critical Abortion Litigation." *Catholic Lawyer* 26 (1981): 178–208.

Hyndman, P. "Refugee Under International Law With a Reference to the Concept of Asylum." *Australian Law Journal* 60 (1986): 148–155.

Illinois Criminal Sexual Assault Act. 1984.

International City Management Association 1989. *The Municipal Yearbook 1989*. Washington, DC: ICMA, 1989.

Jacob, Herbert. "Attorneys for the Public." In *Courts, Law, and Judicial Processes*, edited by S. Ulmer, pp. 82–87. New York: Free Press, 1981.

Johnson, Stephen D., Tamney, Joseph B., and Burton, Ronald. "The Abortion Controversy: Conflicting Beliefs and Values in American Society." Prepared for presentation at the 1990 annual meeting of the American Political Science Association, San Francisco, August 30–September 2, 1990.

Judicial Conference 1983. *Judges of the United States*. Published under the auspices of the Bicentennial Committee of the Judicial Conference of the United States. Washington, DC: U.S. Government Printing Office, 1983.

Karadzole v. Artukovic, 247 F. 2d 198 (9th Cir. 1957) and *United States ex rel. Karadzole v. Artukovic*, 170 F. Supp. 383 (S.D. Cal. 1959).

Kemp, Kathleen A., Carp, Robert A., and Brady, David W. "The Supreme Court and Social Change: The Case of Abortion." *Western Political Quarterly* 31 (1978): 19–31.

Kester, John G. "Some Myths of United States Extradition Law." *Georgetown Law Journal* 76 (1988): 1441.

Krasner, S. D. *Defending the National Interest*. Princeton: Princeton University Press, 1978.

Kritzer, H. "Political Correlates of the Behavior of Federal District Judges." *Journal Of Politics* 40 (1978): 25–57.

LaFree, G. D. *Rape and Criminal Justice*. Belmont, California: Wadsworth, Inc., 1989.

Lawson, K. "Sex Crimes: Revised." *Illinois Issues*: February 1984: 6–11.

Legge, Jerome S., Jr. "The Determinants of Attitudes Toward Abortion in the American Electorate." *Western Political Science Quarterly* 36 (1983): 479–490.

HERRERA, MELODY APRIL

ID:31716000720429
KF3771 .Y37 1995
Copy:1
Abortion politics in
\Yarnold, Barbara M.,
due:3/26/1999,23:59

ID:31716003488388
HQ767.5 .U5 S55
Copy:1
Abortion and alternat
\Skowronski, Marjory,
due:3/26/1999,23:59

ID:31716003383407
HQ767 .G37 1972b
Copy:2
Abortion: the persona
\Gardner, R. F. R. (Re
due:3/26/1999,23:59

ID:31716000238042
HQ767.3 .A25 1988
Copy:1
Abortion and Catholic
\Jung, Patricia Beatti
due:3/26/1999,23:59

ID:31716003580077
HQ767 .A185
Copy:1
Abortion in psychosoc
\David, Henry Philip,
due:3/26/1999,23:59

Levin, Martin A. "Urban Politics and Judicial Behavior." In *American Court Systems*. Edited by S. Goldman and A. Sarat, pp. 338–347. San Francisco: W. H. Freeman and Company, 1978.

Lineberry, R., and Sharkansky, I. *Urban Politics and Public Policy*. New York: Harper & Row, 1978.

Lipsky, Michael. *Street Level Bureaucrats*. New York: Sage Publications, 1980.

Little, Inc., Arthur D. "Determinate and Indeterminate Sentence Law Comparison Study: Feasibility of Adapting Law to a Sentencing Commission-Guideline Approach." San Francisco: Arthur D. Little, Inc., 1980.

Loder, T. *No One But Us*. San Diego: Luramedia, 1986.

Loescher, G., and Scanlan, J. A. *Calculated Kindness*. New York: Free Press, 1986.

Lofland, J. *Deviance and Identity*. Englewood Cliffs, NJ: Prentice-Hall, 1969.

Lowi, Theodore M., Jr. *The End of Liberalism*. New York: W. W. Norton and Company, 1979.

Luker, Kristen. *Abortion and the Politics of Motherhood*. Berkeley: University of California Press, 1984.

Madison, Christopher. "Arab-American Lobby Fights Rearguard Battle to Influence U.S. Mideast Policy." In *Readings In American Government And Politics*, edited by Randall P. Ripley and Elliot E. Slotnick. New York: McGraw-Hill, 1989.

Margolis, M. and Neary, K. "Pressure Politics Revisited: The Anti-Abortion Campaign." *Policy Studies Journal* 8 (1980): 698–716.

Mashaw, J. L. *Due Process in the Administrative State*. New Haven: Yale University Press, 1985.

Mazmanian, D. A., and Sabatier, P. A. *Implementation and Public Policy*. Glenview, IL: Scott, Foresman and Company, 1983.

McConnell, Grant. *Private Power and American Democracy*. New York: Knopf, 1966.

————. "Bringing the War Home." *Basta* (June 1986): 7–14.

McFarland, Andrew S. *Public Interest Lobbies*. Washington, DC: American Enterprise Institute for Public Policy Research, 1980.

————. "Public Interest Lobbies Versus Minority Faction." In *Interest Group Politics*, edited by A. J. Cigler and B. A. Loomis, pp. 324–353. Washington, DC: Congressional Quarterly Press, 1983.

————. "Interest Groups and Theories of Power in America." *British Journal of Political Science* 17 (1987): 129–147.

McRae v. Califano, 491 F. Supp. 630 (1980).

McRae v. Mathews, 421 F. Supp. 533 (1976).

Michigan Department of Corrections 1988. *Annual Report*. Lansing, MI: Michigan Department of Corrections, 1988.

Michigan NOW 1991. Pamphlet. Published by Michigan Conference NOW, Lansing, MI, 1991.

Miethe, T. "Charging and Plea Bargaining Practices Under Determinate Sentences: An Investigation of the Hydraulic Displacement of Discretion." *Journal of Criminal Law and Criminology* 78 (1987): 155–176.

Miller, W., and Stokes, D. "Constituency Influence in Congress." *American Journal of Political Science* 57 (1963): 45–56.

Montana Code Annotated 1988. Helena: Montana Legislative Council, 1988.

Morris, H. "Persons and Punishment." In *Sentencing*, edited by H. Gross and A. Von Hirsch, pp. 93–109. New York: Oxford University Press, 1981.

Murphy, Walter F. "Courts as Small Groups." In *Courts, Law, and Judicial Processes*, edited by S. S. Ulmer, pp. 363–367. New York: Free Press, 1981.

Myers, M. "Economic Inequality and Discrimination in Sentencing." *Social Forces* 65 (1987): 746–766.

_____. "Social Background and the Sentencing Behavior of Judges." *Criminology* 26 (1988): 649–673.

Nagel, I., and Hagan, J. "Gender and Crime: Offense Patterns and Criminal Court Sanctions." *Crime and Justice: Annual Review of Research* 4 (1983): 91–144.

Nagel, Stuart S. "Political Party Affiliation and Judges' Decisions." *American Political Science Review* 55 (1961): 843–850.

National Federation of Temple Sisterhoods. Resolutions adopted by the National Federation of Temple Sisterhoods at the 38th Biennial Assembly, October 31–November 4, 1991, Baltimore MD. Resolution IX: Women's Health Care, Resolution 5, pp. 19–20. Published by the Department on Religious Action, The National Federation of Temple Sisterhoods, New York, 1991.

National Lawyers Guild 1986. *Central America Refugee Defense Fund Newsletter*. June 6, 1986.

National Right to Life 1990. *Annual Report 1990*. National Right to Life Educational Trust Fund. Washington, DC, 1990.

Newman, D. J. "Perspectives of Probation: Legal Issues and Professional Trends." In *The Challenge Of Change In The Correctional Process*, pp. 7–8. Hackensack, NJ: The National Council on Crime and Delinquency, 1972.

Newman, D. J. and Anderson, P. R. *Introduction to Criminal Justice*. New York: Random House, 1989.

Noonan, John. *A Private Choice: Abortion in America in the Seventies*. New York: Free Press, 1979.

NOW 1990. *1990 Annual Report*. National Organization for Women Legal Defense and Education Fund. New York: 1990.

O'Connor, K. *Women's Organizations Use of the Courts*. Lexington: Lexington Books, 1980.

O'Connor, K., and Epstein, L. "The Rise of Conservative Interest Group Litigation." *Journal of Politics* 45 (1983): 479–489.

O'Leary, V., Gottfredson, M., and Gelman, A. "Contemporary Sentencing Proposals." *Criminal Law Bulletin* 11 (1975): 555–586.

Olson, Mancur. *The Logic of Collective Action*. Boston: Harvard University Press, 1971.

Page, B. I., Shapiro, R. Y., Gronke, P. W., and Rosenberg, R. M. "Constituency, Party, and Representation in Congress." *Public Opinion Quarterly* 48 (1984): 741–756.

Parker, Karen. "Human Rights and Humanitarian Law." *Whittier Law Review* 7 (1985): 675–681.

Petchesky, Rosalind. "Antiabortion, Antifeminism and the Rise of the New Right." *Feminist Studies* 7 (1981): 206–246.

_____. *Abortion and Woman's Choice*. New York: Longman, 1984.

Peterson, Ruth, and Hagan, J. "Changing Conceptions of Race: Towards an Account of Anomalous Findings of Sentencing Research." *American Sociological Review* 49 (1984): 56–70.

Pindyck, R., and Rubinfeld, D. *Econometric Models and Econometric Forecasts*. New York: McGraw-Hill, 1981.

Pious, Richard. *The American Presidency*. New York: Basic Books, 1979.

PPLA 1990. *1990 Annual Report*. Planned Parenthood/World Population of Los Angeles. Los Angeles, 1990.

Preston, R. K. "Asylum Adjudications: Do State Department Advisory Opinions Violate Refugees' Rights and United States International Obligations?" *Maryland Law Review* 45 (1986): 91–140.

Pritchett, C. Herman. "Voting Behavior on the United States Supreme Court." In *American Court Systems*, edited by S. Goldman and A. Sarat, pp. 424–431. San Francisco: W. H. Freeman and Company, 1978.

Quinn v. Robinson, No. C-82-6688 PPA (N.D. Cal. 1983).

Refugee Act of 1980, Public Law No. 96-212, 96th Cong., 2d Sess., March 17, 1980.

Richardson, R. J., and Vines, K. N. "Judicial Constituencies: The Politics of Structure." In *American Court Systems*, edited by S. Goldman and A. Sarat, pp. 348–353. San Francisco: W. H. Freeman and Company, 1978.

Ripley, Randall B., Slotnick, Elliot E. *Readings in American Government and Politics*. New York: McGraw-Hill, 1989.

Robinson, J., and Smith, G. "The Effectiveness of Correctional Programs." In *Sentencing*, edited by H. Gross and A. Von Hirsch, pp. 118–129. New York: Oxford University Press, 1981.

Roe v. Wade, 410 U.S. 113 (1973).

Rosenbloom, David H. *Public Administration*. New York: Random House, 1989.

Rosenne, Shabtai. *The World Court*. Dobbs Ferry, NY: A. W. Sijthoff-Leiden, Oceana Publications, 1973.

Rothman, D. J. "Decarcerating Prisoners and Patients." In *Sentencing*, edited by H. Gross and A. Von Hirsch, pp. 130–147. New York: Oxford University Press, 1981.

Rutherford 1990. Information pamphlet. Published by The Rutherford Institute, Charlottesville, VA, 1990.

Sackett, Victoria A. "Between Pro-Life and Pro-Choice." *Public Opinion* 8 (1985): 53–55.

Schattshneider, E. E. *The Semisovereign People*. New York: Holt, Rinehart and Winston, 1960.

Schlozman, K. L. and Tierney, J. T. *Organized Interests and American Democracy*. New York: Harper & Row, 1986.

Schmidhauser, A. S. "The Social and Political Backgrounds of the Justices of the Supreme Court: 1789–1959." In *American Court Systems*, edited by S. Goldman and A. Sarat, pp. 280–289. San Francisco: W. H. Freeman and Company, 1978.

Schubert, G. *The Judicial Mind*. Evanston, IL: Northwestern University Press, 1965.

Schur, E. *Labeling Deviant Behavior: Its Sociological Implications*. New York: Harper & Row, 1971.

Scott, Jacqueline. *Conflicting Values and Compromise Beliefs About Abortion*. Ph.D. Dissertation, University of Michigan, University Microfilms International, 1987.

Scott, Jacqueline, and Schuman, Howard. "Attitude Strength and Social Action in the Abortion Dispute." *American Sociological Review* 53 (1988): 785–793.

Segal, J. "Predicting Supreme Court Cases Probabilistically: The Search and Seizure Cases 1962–1981." *American Political Science Review* 78 (1984): 891–900.

Segal, Jeffrey A. "Measuring Change on the Supreme Court: Examining Alternative Models." *American Journal of Political Science* 29 (1985): 461–479.

Segers, Mary C. "Can Congress Settle the Abortion Issue?" *Hastings Center Report* 12 (1982): 20–28.

Simon, H. A. *Administrative Behavior*. New York: MacMillan Company, 1957.

Simon, H. A., Smithburg, D. W., and Thompson, V. A. *Public Administration*. New York: Knopf, 1962.

Sobrino, J. "Theological Analysis of the Sanctuary Movement." *Basta* (June 1987) 19–24.

Spaeth, Harold J. "The Attitudes and Values of Supreme Court Justices." In *Courts, Law, and Judicial Processes*, edited by S. S. Ulmer, pp. 387–397. New York: Frcc Press, 1981.

Spencer, C. C. "Sexual Assault: The Second Victimization." In *Women, The Courts, and Equality*, edited by L. Crites and W. Hepperle. Beverly Hills: Sage Publications, 1978.

Spohn, C., Gruhl, J., and Welch, Susan. "The Effects of Race on Sentencing: A Re-Examination of an Unsettled Question." *Law And Society Review* 16 (1981–1982): 71–88.

Sprague, J. D. *Voting Patterns of the U.S. Supreme Court*. New York: Bobbs-Merrill Co., 1968.

State of Montana Supreme Court 1988. *Montana Courts: 1988 Judicial Report*. Helena, MT, 1988.

Steel, R. D. *Steel on Immigration Law*. San Francisco: Bancroft-Whitney Co., 1985.

Steffensmeier, D., and Kramer, J. H. "Sex-Based Differences in the Sentencing of Adult Criminal Defendants: An Empirical Test and Theoretical Overview." *Sociology And Social Research: An International Journal* 66 (1982): 289–304.

Stokes, D. "Spatial Models of Party Competition." *American Political Science Review* 57 (1963): 368–377.

Tanenhaus, J. "Supreme Court Attitudes Toward Federal Administrative Agencies 1947–1956—An Application of Social Science Methods to the Study of Judicial Process." *Vanderbilt Law Review* 14 (1961): 482–501.

Tanenhaus, J., Schick, M., Muraskin, M., and Rosen, D. "The Supreme Court's Certiorari Jurisdiction: Cue Theory." In *Courts, Law, and Judicial Processes*, edited by S. S. Ulmer, pp. 273–283. New York: Free Press, 1981.

Tatalovich, R., and Daynes, B. W. *The Politics of Abortion*. New York: Praeger Publishers, 1981.

Tate, C. Neal. "Personal Attributes as Explanations of Supreme Court Justices' Decision Making." In *Courts in American Politics*, edited by H. R. Glick, pp. 266–275. New York: McGraw-Hill, 1990.

The Economist. "The Fearful Politics of Abortion." 312 (July 8, 1989): 21–23.

Turk, A. *Criminality and Legal Order*. Rand McNally and Company, 1969.

————. *Legal Sanctioning and Social Control*. Washington, DC: Government Printing Office, 1972.

Ulmer, S. Sidney. *Courts, Law, and Judicial Processes*. New York: Free Press, 1981.

Ungs, T. D., and Bass, L. R. "Judicial Role Perceptions: A Q-Technique Study of Ohio Judges." *Law and Society Review* 6 (1972): 343–366.

Unnever, J., and Hembroff, L. "The Prediction of Racial/Ethnic Sentencing Disparities: An Expectation States Approach." *Journal of Research in Crime and Delinquency* 25 (1988): 53–82.

U.S. Bureau of the Census 1988. *County and City Data Book.* Washington, DC: U.S. Government Printing Office, 1988.

———. *Historical Statistics of the United States: Colonial Time to 1970.* Part 1. Washington, DC: U.S. Government Printing Office, 1975.

———. *Seventeenth U.S. Census*, Special Reports, Nativity and Parentage, Volume IV, Part 3, Ch. A, Table 12, pp. 3A-71-74. Washington, DC: U.S. Government Printing Office, 1954.

———. *State and Metropolitan Area Data Book.* Washington, DC: U.S. Government Printing Office, 1986.

———. *Statistical Abstract of the United States: 1982–83.* Washington, DC: U.S. Government Printing Office, 1982.

U.S. Department of Justice 1984. *1984 Statistical Yearbook of the Immigration and Naturalization Service.* Washington, DC, 1984.

U.S. Department of Labor 1980–1987. *Employment and Earnings.* Washington, DC, 1987.

Van Der Hout, M. "The Politics of Asylum." *California Lawyer* 5 (1985): 72.

Vines, Kenneth N. "The Role of Circuit Courts of Appeal in the Federal Judicial Process: A Case Study." *Midwest Journal of Political Science* 7 (1963): 305–319.

———. "Federal District Judges and Race Relations Cases in the South." In *American Court Systems*, edited by S. Goldman and A. Sarat, pp. 376–385. San Francisco: W. H. Freeman and Company, 1978.

Von Hirsch, Andrew. *Past or Future Crimes.* New Brunswick, NJ: Rutgers University Press, 1987.

Vose, Clement E. *Caucasions Only.* Berkeley: Knopf, 1959.

———. "Litigation as a Form of Pressure Group Activity." In *Courts in American Politics*, edited by Henry R. Glick, pp. 67–72. New York: McGraw-Hill, 1990.

Walker, Jack L. "The Origins and Maintenance of Interest Groups in America." *American Political Science Review* 127 (1983): 390–406.

Walker, T. G. "A Note Concerning Partisan Influence On Trial-Judge Decision Making." *Law And Society Review* 6 (1972): 645–649.

Wall, D. "Michigan Supreme Court and Court of Appeals Election." Paper presented at Midwest Political Science Association, 1985.

Wenner, Lettie M. *The Environmental Decade in Court.* Bloomington, IN: Indiana University Press, 1982.

Wenner, Lettie M. and Dutter, Lee. "Contextual Influences on Court Outcomes." *Western Political Quarterly* 41 (1988): 115–134.

Williams, K., and Drake, S. "Social Structure, Crime and Criminalization: An
Empirical Examination of the Conflict Perspective." *The Sociological Quarterly* 21 (1980): 563–575.

Williams, K., and Timberlake, M. "Structured Inequality, Conflict, and Control: A Cross-National Test of the Threat Hypothesis." *Social Forces* 63
(1984): 414–432.

Wolpert, Robin, and Rosenberg, Gerald N. "The Least Dangerous Branch:
Market Forces and the Implementation of Roe." Prepared for delivery at the
1990 annual meeting of the American Political Science Association, San
Francisco, August 30–September 2, 1990.

Women's Division. *United Methodist Women: In the Middle of Tomorrow.*
Centennial Supplement Edition by Barbara E. Campbell (1975) and Supple-
ment (1983) published by the Women's Division of the Board of Global
Ministries of the United Methodist Church. New York City, 1975.

Woodman, Sue. "Reproductive Rights." *New Statesman & Society* 2 (August
18, 1989): 20–21.

Woodward, Howard, J., Jr. "Role Perceptions and Behavior in Three
U.S. Courts of Appeals." In *American Court Systems*, edited by S. Goldman
and A. Sarat, pp. 480–489. San Francisco: W. H. Freeman and Company,
1978.

Yarnold, Barbara M. 1990a. "Federal Court Outcomes In Asylum-Related
Appeals 1980–1987: A Highly 'Politicized' Process." *Policy Sciences.* 23
(November 1990): 291–306.

_____. 1990b. *Refugees Without Refuge: Formation and Failed Implementa-
tion of U.S. Political Asylum Policy in the 1980s.* Lanham, MD: University
Press of America, 1990.

_____. 1990c. "The Refuge Act of 1980 and the De-Politicization of
Refugee/Asylum Admissions: An Example of Failed Policy Implementation." *American Politics Quarterly* 18 (October 1990): 527–536.

_____. "United States Refugee and Asylum Policy: Factors that Impact
Legislative, Administrative and Judicial Decisions." Ph.D. Dissertation,
University of Illinois at Chicago, 1988.

_____. 1991a. *International Fugitives: A New Role for the International
Court of Justice.* New York: Praeger Publishers, Inc., 1991.

_____. 1991b. "The Role of Religious Organizations in the U.S. Sanctuary
Movement." In *The Role of Religious Organizations in Social Movements*,
edited by Barbara M. Yarnold. New York: Praeger Publishers, 1991.

_____. 1992a. *Politics and the Courts: Toward a General Theory of Public
Law.* New York: Praeger Publishers, 1992.

Zatz, M. "The Changing Forms of Racial/Ethnic Biases in Sentencing." *Journal of Research in Crime and Delinquency* 24 (1987): 69–92.

Zimring, F. "Making the Punishment Fit the Crime: A Consumers' Guide to Sentencing Reform." In *Sentencing*, edited by H. Gross and A. Von Hirsch, pp. 327–335. New York: Oxford University Press, 1981.

INDEX

ABOUT THE AUTHOR

Barbara M. Yarnold is an attorney and has practiced in the areas of immigration and corporate law, among others. She is currently an assistant professor of public administration at Florida International University. She is also the author of *Refugees Without Refuge, International Fugitives: A New Role for the International Court of Justice*, and *Politics and the Courts: Toward a General Theory of Public Law*, and editor of *The Role of Religious Organizations in Social Movements*.